Finding Our Balance

Finding Our Balance

Repositioning Mainstream Protestantism

RONALD P. BYARS

with a Foreword by Thomas W. Currie

CASCADE *Books* • Eugene, Oregon

FINDING OUR BALANCE
Repositioning Mainstream Protestantism

Copyright © 2015 Ronald P. Byars. All rights reserved. Except for brief quotations in critical publications or reviews, no part of this book may be reproduced in any manner without prior written permission from the publisher. Write: Permissions, Wipf and Stock Publishers, 199 W. 8th Ave., Suite 3, Eugene, OR 97401.

Cascade Books
An imprint of Wipf and Stock Publishers
199 W. 8th Ave., Suite 3
Eugene, OR 97401

www.wipfandstock.com

ISBN: 978-1-4982-0024-0

Cataloging-in Publication data:

    Byars, Ronald P.

    Finding our balance : repositioning mainstream Protestantism / Ronald P. Byars ; foreword by Thomas W. Currie.

    xiv + 124 p. ; cm. Includes bibliographical references.

    ISBN: 978-1-4982-0024-0

    1. Protestant churches—United States. 2. Protestant churches—North America. 3. Christianity—21st century. I. Currie, Thomas W. II. Title.

BR121.3 B93 2015

Manufactured in the U.S.A.

Unless otherwise noted, the Scripture quotations in this publication are from the New Revised Standard Version of the Bible, copyright © 1989 by the Division of Christian Education of the National Council of Churches of Christ in the U.S.A.

For Susan Rhodes Byars

PREVIOUS BOOKS BY RONALD P. BYARS

Christian Worship: Glorifying and Enjoying God

The Future of Protestant Worship: Beyond the Worship Wars

The Bread of Life: A Guide to the Lord's Supper for Presbyterians

Lift Your Hearts on High: Eucharistic Prayer in the Reformed Tradition

What Language Shall I Borrow? The Bible and Christian Worship

The Sacraments in Biblical Perspective

Come and See: Presbyterian Congregations Celebrating Weekly Communion

Contents

Foreword by Thomas W. Currie / ix

Acknowledgments xiii

Introduction: Where Are We, and How Did We Get Here? 1

PART 1

1. Question *which* Authority? 17
2. What's the Matter with Orthodoxy? 38

PART 2

3. Mid-American Generic Protestant Worship 59
4. What's at Stake on Sunday Morning? 77
5. Attentiveness to the Poor: Revisiting the Protestant Ethic 96

Epilogue 115

A Sermon Preached at First Presbyterian Church, Lexington, Kentucky 117

Bibliography 123

Foreword

Ron Byars thinks the church should abandon its principles and embrace its faith. When uprooted from the church's affirmation concerning Jesus Christ, the "Protestant principle" of refusing to absolutize any creed, doctrine, or ecclesiastical practice, becomes a kind of absolute itself, trivializing the message of the gospel and emptying it of any real substance. As a result, a culture that is only too comfortable with the absoluteness of its own self-chosen certainties will remain quite unoffended, and worse, uninspired by the moralistic timidity of another bland "absolute."

What Byars sees is a church that wants to be committed to the principles of inclusiveness, hospitality, and tolerance, without the burden of affirming the heart of the Christian faith, a faith that is scandalously particular and painfully distinct from virtues or values that the culture often prizes. A more "principled" Christianity will always appear to be a bloodless thing, uncomfortable with doctrinal specificity, and unable to call into question the culture's deepest certainties or its most self-evident truths. Trying to preach the gospel without doctrine, he thinks, is like trying to preach the Word without the flesh, or like trying to tell a story without a plot, or worse, like trying to explain a joke. The explanation always falls flat. It is the joke that is funny, not the explanation. For this reason, efforts to proclaim an undoctrinal Christianity always result in a faith that is "doctrinal" in the worst sense, that is, a faith that is full of "principles" that are pressed into service to do the work of the Word made flesh, an impossible task, and one that is as boring as it is joyless.

Jesus Christ is not an ideal or a principle or aspiration. He is a person, and the claims about him are extraordinary, even scandalous: God in human flesh; the risen and living Lord; the One in whom all things hold together; the head whose body makes a communion of believers throughout the world; the one true human from whose life we receive our own humanity; the way, the truth, and the life. It is not easy to smooth over these claims. They are difficult to ignore, much less to exchange for a set of more accessible principles.

The appeal to some "higher principle" above the stubborn particularities of the faith is not new. That was essentially Erasmus's advice to Luther in the sixteenth century. Why quibble over doctrine, Erasmus asked, or even over the institutional church? Theological convictions are not worth quarreling over; they are nothing more than the opinions of philosophers at any given time. Divine things are above us anyway; we should not let our doctrines disturb the equanimity or peace of the faith. Rather, we should emphasize the moral nature of the Christian life, do our good works, and content ourselves with simple prayers and quiet faith. But Luther disagreed, and he disagreed not because he was looking for a fight but because he thought Erasmus's notion of "peace" emptied the faith of any genuine content, offering a nihilistic stone to those looking for bread. The Holy Spirit, Luther wrote, is not a skeptic, and the affirmations of the faith are not mere opinions or doubtful aspirations but claims that are more firm than life itself. What would the faith be without the claim that God was in Christ reconciling the world? What would the faith be without the claim that Jesus is Lord—not the Almighty Dollar, not my political convictions, not some self-constructed identity? Those idols are, well, excluded, and they are excluded not on the basis of some superior principle but on the basis of what God has done and is doing in Jesus Christ.

To be really critical, to embrace the kinds of questions that truly question established authority, one must have a basis on which to stand. The myth that this book so ably exposes is the notion that one can question authority without such a basis and without having one's own position questioned. Byars knows that none of our questions and none of our principles are neutral things. They all are rooted in affirmations of one sort or another, often in nothing more than a kind of self-affirmation. Which is why it is always dangerous to read Scripture, because there we are encountered by the God who questions us, questions even our vaunted "principles." The church can only adopt an Erasmian "peace" by avoiding Scripture's witness to the God who meets us in Jesus Christ. A church that seeks to save itself by insulating itself from such questions, perhaps in the hopes of earning some kind of credibility with the culture, is a church that is simultaneously cutting itself off from its deepest and richest resources while at the same time rendering itself boringly like the very culture it is hoping to impress. So does salt soon lose its savor.

This book does more, however, than question our culture's and our church's questions. It also helps us see some rich gifts clothed in old garb which we have too easily dismissed. Byars thinks words like *liturgy*, *orthodox*, *catholic*, and *creed* have much to teach us and need to be rediscovered by the church today, in part because they provide a richer and more sustaining witness than our disembodied ideals and earnest exhortations. Even the vital calling of the church to care for the poor is a gift and a task more deeply rooted in the gospel's own narrative and more powerfully sustained in the liturgy of the church's own worship than in the various principles and solutions proposed by a consumer culture. Getting better acquainted with the church's historic language is crucial for understanding and undertaking its mission to the world. Hidden in these ancient terms are gifts that will make the church's proclamation a more compelling enterprise, and will convey some of the liberating joy (and mystery) that the gospel regularly insists on giving the world.

The most remarkable thing about this book is its affirmative character. Byars finds himself located in a tradition that is refreshingly unworried about some things. It is not worried about its own survival. It is not worried about gaining the approval of the "cultured among the despisers of religion." It is not even worried about the myriad of ways the church fails to be the church. The tradition that has nourished Byars and which he seeks to pass on to us is convinced that Jesus Christ is the one particular that both causes us to stumble and gathers us into life-giving communion. It is to him that we are to entrust our worship, our principles, and our lives. He has liberated us from every effort to save ourselves, even the most high-minded. To be liberated by him is, as the Pharisees learned and the disciples of every age have had to discover as well, to be set free from the broad yet boring path of the law and to be set free for the joyful if humbling adventure of life in Christ. Such a life is always a life together, and this book carefully traces the lineaments of that life in calling us to embrace the One who draws us into it.

To read this book is to sense the call to discipleship, to be given the words to describe its mysterious path, to see the dimensions of the life it unfolds, and to rejoice in this journey as if one could finally espy one's true home. Gospel stories do that for us, whether we be prodigals lost in a far country or elder brothers lost in a more principled distant land, offended by the music audible from a joyful homecoming. This book helps us hear that music. To read it is to discern the grace notes coming from that great banquet celebration that is Christ's own life, a kind of music that is able to draw us all the way home.

Thomas W. Currie
Union Presbyterian Seminary, Charlotte Campus
Ascension Day 2014

Acknowledgments

THANKS TO DAVID MAXWELL, Ron Luckey, and Joe R. Jones for reading early drafts of various chapters in the book and offering their encouragement. Of course, they are not to be held responsible for my opinions.

Introduction
Where Are We, and How Did We Get Here?

WE ARE LIVING, AS far as any sort of religious faith is concerned, in a time of cultural and spiritual crisis. And yet, if one visits services in American Protestant churches, it is not always clear whether anyone in charge has noticed the crisis. The crisis, like nearly all crises, poses a theological challenge. Not just, or even primarily, a challenge to academic theology, but one that is more pressing: a challenge to the theology that animates congregations, the sort that cries out to be embedded in preaching and worship. The challenge to those who preach is one that requires discovering speech adequate to express the deepest affirmations of the church's faith in ways accessible to the minds and hearts of people whose daily lives expose them to often benign but powerful antitheses to the gospel. And the challenge is also to those who plan services—that liturgies may be rooted deeply enough in the church's ecosystem to give life to the wonderfully rich affirmations of the gospel. These sorts of challenges cannot be met by business as usual. All churches are in trouble, and mid-American, generic Protestantism is in trouble in its own way. Some of that trouble stems from stumbling attempts to adjust to cultural change, and some results from anachronisms in thought and practice. It is time for a serious conversation—indeed, for a rethinking of some things we have taken for granted, and a consequent repositioning with respect to the prevailing culture.

Thanks for the Memory: Cultural Hegemony

Those who have long memories can recall a time when the churches were full, when new ones were opening, when building projects were being initiated, and when it was presumed that nearly everyone was either a church member or ought to be. The full sanctuaries of the post–World War II period represented, in large part, a reaction to the political and social situation of the era. Once the war had been won, the Soviet Union, our temporary ally during the war, became a serious and intimidating competitor. The threat of nuclear annihilation at the push of a button made praying to a benevolent God seem a prudent thing to do. The frightening specter of "godless Communism" seemed to require Americans to identify themselves, by contrast, as a "godly" people. Becoming a member of a worshiping community clarified the distinction between these two diametrically opposed ways of life. And it did not hurt that the growing suburban developments that began to spring up everywhere in peacetime created an appetite for the kind of postwar relationship building and community building that churches were well-equipped to offer.

Does that mean that the religious "revival" of the 1950s was not genuine but only a social and political phenomenon? Not necessarily. Neither intellectual curiosity about religion nor an honest piety needs to be walled off from whatever is going on in the world. The social environment of that era simply served as a catalyst that had the effect of turning some people's thoughts and minds toward what might be called heavenly things. While many, no doubt, simply followed the herd into the churches, others did find themselves genuinely drawn to the Christian gospel.

However, at no time in the twentieth century, neither before nor after the war, did members of the so-called mainline churches ever number more than 20 percent of the U.S. population.[1] The temporary phenomenon of swelling numbers in the mainline (or "oldline") churches after the Second World War was an anomaly and did not last long, but it is burned into the memory of many who remember it as though it constitutes a baseline that ought to be the norm for all time.

The Authority in Numbers

For anyone who came of age in the 1960s or later, it may be difficult to comprehend the authoritative role of mainline religion in the 1950s. I say "mainline *religion*" because the chief identifiers were Protestant, Catholic, and Jewish. Protestant evangelicals and fundamentalists had been effectively sidelined both intellectually and popularly after the Scopes trial and

---

1. Campbell, *Glory Days?*, 12.

ecclesiastical battles that ended with the discrediting of biblical literalism. Class issues were at work, raising the profile of the primarily middle- and upper-class mainline and distinguishing them from Pentecostals and evangelicals, who were, at the time, less educated and more likely from socially and economically marginalized classes; so the old-line, traditional Protestant churches were the ones with the high profile. Roman Catholics had made serious progress in assimilating to the dominant culture but still maintained an identity marked by a lingering sense of being a besieged minority, so Catholics were inclined to be on the defensive. The term *Judeo-Christian* had become popular, and its prevalence indicated that Jewishness was no longer considered alien to an American identity, particularly in an era that contrasted the godly with godless Communists; but Jewish people still understood that they were not entirely part of the mainstream. In any case, although Protestantism was presumed to be the norm, to be religious was nevertheless good enough in an era when the most important contrast was with atheistic Communism.

If in the 1950s the default setting in American society was to be religious in one form or another, the '50s were also an era in which the order of the day was to "have faith in faith," without, as President Eisenhower suggested, necessarily exercising too much discrimination in the matter.[2] Hollywood studios, sensing a marketing opportunity, produced popularly focused movies with religious themes, like *Quo Vadis* (1951) and *The Ten Commandments* (1956), and even a popular movie about a preacher, *A Man Called Peter* (1955).

Here is what it looked like: Almost everybody was expected to be able to identify a "religious preference" if necessary. When filling out a form that asked for such a preference, those who were neither Jewish nor Catholic nor an adherent of some other specific religion (a rare case) were expected to mark "Protestant," whether they had ever set foot in a church or not. Authority figures went to church: schoolteachers, principals, mayors, the president of the United States, congressional representatives, Senators, owners or CEOs of businesses large and small, doctors, lawyers, faculty members of Ivy League colleges, military officers, writers, actors—in short, anybody you can think of who occupied any position that gave them the appearance

---

2. "Our government has no sense unless it is founded in a deeply felt religious faith, and I don't care what it is." Eisenhower said this in 1952 after meeting Soviet Marshal Grigori Zhukov. Eisenhower's remark may not do justice to the seriousness of his own religious faith, but "I don't care what it is" surely represents a characteristic way of thinking in this early Cold War period.

of any kind of authority. Battell Chapel at Yale University was packed on Sundays with students, faculty, and the president of the university, and the university chaplain occupied a high-profile position in the larger community as well as on campus. Even in summertime, when Sunday university worship occurred in a smaller chapel, the president was there even though it is not likely that anyone was keeping track.

The mainline churches were the primary benefactors of the attention and aspirations of these various figures of authority. The opinions of mainline church leaders and theologians were taken seriously. People who did not count themselves among the pious were among those who read theologians like Paul Tillich and, particularly, Reinhold Niebuhr.

Young people coming to maturity in the 1950s were immersed in a culture that by and large viewed religious faith in a positive light and granted it both authority and social support. Christian youth and student movements were strong and appealing. Denominational treasuries were full and the churches planning new buildings to accommodate all the people. This was in the last days of an era when institutions were normally respected, including religious institutions, and the press and other media tended to approach them with kid gloves.

Pushback: Cultural Change

In short, religious faith, particularly mainline Protestantism both in its popular and its intellectual forms, was considered worthy of participation in the cultural and intellectual marketplace, and even capable of projecting a prophetic edge. As the 1950s morphed into the 1960s, the mainline churches provided a good deal of active participation and even leadership in the civil rights movement and other progressive causes. As the '60s progressed, the conservative backlash against cultural change often included attacks on the mainline churches, and particularly on the National and World Councils of Churches, both of which were seen by conservatives as too politically liberal—out of touch with conventional values and too sympathetic to minority voices.

Nevertheless, the 1960s saw the emergence of a mainstream culture in which institutions of every sort began to be held in deep suspicion. After all, the apparently benign institutions of American society—whether government, business, educational or religious institutions—seemed for generations to have condoned or at least been indifferent to segregation, racism, sexism, and other injustices that permeated the whole culture. The civil rights movement, the Vietnam War, and the Watergate scandal, among other phenomena, contributed to public skepticism and to the encouragement of investigative journalism. A whole generation was formed to be skeptical of established institutions of every kind, and that skepticism struck a blow that left a permanent legacy even when the Baby Boomers eventually shed their revolutionary postures and made their peace with commercial and celebrity culture.

American churches, particularly those of the Protestant so-called mainline, had occupied a position of status and privilege since before the founding of the republic, even in periods when actual members of those churches were in the minority. American Protestants were among the most recent heirs of the post-Constantinian settlement, when the conversion of the Roman emperor to Christianity ensured the church a privileged position in what became European society. Being in a position of privilege and status suggested authority, so that people simply presumed that Christianity should be the default setting for the spiritual lives of Western people. When that privileged status evaporated, diminishing with particular force in the 1960s, that authority-by-default disappeared. It was clear that Christianity was one religion among others, with no special claim to anyone's allegiance simply because they were Americans, or because they or their family had had some sort of affiliation with a church in times past.

The Loss of Authority

In the new, twenty-first century, the child-abuse crisis in the Roman Catholic Church as well as the rise of the Religious Right and militant Islam invited the kind of journalistic exposure and social disgust that marked a definitive end to any special treatment for religious bodies or institutions. While in an earlier era the term *Christianity* implied the familiar mainline churches, by the new century it was far more likely to be identified with groups that opposed the teaching of evolution in public schools, that advocated posting the Ten Commandments in courthouses and other public places, and that contended for prayers at meetings of secular governing bodies, while the former mainline receded into near invisibility. With public respect for the church and its faith flagging, Americans began to feel free to vent their negative experiences with churches, and free as well to explore options near and far, religious or otherwise, with no sense of obligation to the previously established order. By the end of the first decade of the new century, the default setting, when it came to religious faith, was skepticism, marked by a steady statistical increase in the numbers of those who claimed to have no religious affiliation at all.

"When did faith start to fade?" asks Adam Gopnik in an essay in the *New Yorker*. From Tom Stoppard's play *Jumpers*, Gopnik quotes a character who says, "There is presumably a calendar date—a *moment*—when the onus of proof passed from the atheist to the believer, when, quite suddenly, the noes had it."[3] Obviously, from the standpoint of the early twenty-first century, the culture of the 1950s seems not only immensely distant but almost the diametric opposite of contemporary experience, since what had been taken as authoritative in the '50s and for generations before has—suddenly, it seems—been turned upside down. Since cultural authority has shifted in favor of the skeptics (at least among those who are most attuned to the *Zeitgeist*), those who strive to keep up with cultural trends tend to defer, as always, to the prevailing consensus.

True, many Americans continue to feel some sort of loyalty to their churches, or to the idea of church, and congregational life continues more or less as usual. However, the question of authority hangs over the church in a way that it had not for generations. When the neighbors, the role models, the heavy-lifting intellectuals, the celebrities, and almost everybody you know no longer goes to church, the average person finds every good reason not to discern any authority in ecclesiastical quarters either. A religious identity that once seemed easy, natural, and popular is no longer. The cultural authority granted to the church has been withdrawn, and social support for religious faith is rapidly evaporating. The reputation of the Roman Catholic Church has crumbled from both within and without. Protestantism is in disarray, scarcely identifiable as a single entity. *Protestant* has become a generic label that can be applied to a wide spectrum of radically different bodies as well as independent congregations and parachurch groups. The former mainline is invisible to the media and traumatized by the high profile of the Religious Right. Those who continue their allegiance to the now sidelined mainline churches can easily fall into a kind of self-pity: *Nobody likes us anymore!*

---

3. Gopnik, "Bigger Than Phil," 107.

Now what shall we do?

One way of dealing with the mainline crisis is denial. In other words, we simply carry on the way we are used to as though nothing has changed, hoping the tide will turn once again. Another way of dealing with the crisis is to entertain experiments in creativity. Some of these, like the baby-boomer-inspired "seeker services," become almost ubiquitous, the surefire solution to every congregation's problem drawing people younger than the majority of their constituents (until they don't draw them anymore). Other proposed solutions come and go, the more radical or offbeat sometimes catching a bit of attention in the newspapers or church publications for a time. No doubt pragmatism has a role to play when trying to imagine unconventional means of evangelizing the unchurched or arousing the enthusiasm of those who haven't left yet, but it is apparent that there is no recipe, no silver bullet, that will simply reverse the setbacks of the church if only they were to be widely implemented. In any case, even a pragmatically based experiment needs to be rooted in something bigger than the desire to draw a crowd. One may cheer those who devote their energies and imaginations to finding new ways, but it is important not to neglect addressing some basic questions: What is the goal? Is it to increase our numbers? Retain the constituencies we still have? Increase social respect and public influence? Exhibit as vividly and authentically as possible the appeal and promise of the gospel of Jesus Christ? All of these? None of them?

The old-line churches, desperate, on the one hand, to distance themselves from hard-right fundamentalism and, on the other, to adopt a respectful acknowledgment of their own cultural demotion, seem to have lost their theological nerve, earnestly trying to blend in to a post-Christian society. Disturbed and bewildered by their changed circumstances, mainline churches face the temptation to soft-pedal the bolder affirmations of classic Christianity so as to cause no offense to constituents who share the larger culture's about-face. A common result is to find ourselves playing in the shallow end of the pool, mirroring conventional pieties about spirituality, about boosting self-esteem, and about enhancing self-fulfillment, as though these were the point of the gospel rather than possible side-effects. That route certainly leads to a dead end.

Presuming that the post-Constantinian era is over, it is probably futile to imagine that we can reverse the tide. It may be more helpful to take the pre-Constantine era for our model, when the infant church was decidedly in the minority among all sorts of religious movements and competing values. In that period Christians did not imagine that they would enjoy special privilege in society, and proceeded to nurture their communal life and values according to their own inner logic and imperatives, without expecting public attention or acclamation. No doubt those Christians before Constantine took seriously the dominical charge to go "into all the world, making disciples," but they were not accustomed to the expectation that they would necessarily win converts in large numbers or manage sizeable institutions of their own, while we today are constantly reminded of our earlier cultural hegemony by the need to care for existing buildings, support professional staff, and provide financial stability for various institutions and projects created out of our commitment to mission and service over the generations. Our situation is clearly different from both the Constantinian and pre-Constantinian eras, but there may be wisdom in paying more attention to the time when Christianity was one possibility among many, reaching out vigorously, but not tied in knots by expectations of occupying a privileged position in society. If we choose to take that period as our model, we will find that the New Testament speaks to us more pointedly than when we imagine ourselves to have been granted the privilege of being in charge of the spiritual life of a whole society.

Reconsidering Our Position

I am not advocating that we withdraw from the world or turn away from the responsibility of engaging with the larger society, but just turning indiscriminately to any strategy or promotion that may possibly strengthen our public image cannot bypass the need for a theological foundation. A better idea is that we, like our early predecessors, learn to nurture our communal life and values according to their inner logic and imperatives. In other words, we would be wise not to be distracted by thinking, first of all, about numbers or influence or maintaining a lost ecclesiastical empire. Rather we would be wiser to bring into sharper focus the gospel handed on to us, one that has theological and ethical content with personal, communal, and social implications. Let us devote ourselves to that first, and then let the numbers fall where they may. The church, after all, is a community built on faith in the resurrection of the Lord. The resurrection was not an achievement that sprang out of a determination not ever, ever to be defeated, but rather a gift made manifest in that One who did not choose to launch a fierce defensive battle to save his own life. To try to save our institutional life as it is, at all costs, is a worthless endeavor that is likely to end in the loss of the very thing God called the church into being to preserve and advance.

The issue would seem to be the challenge of studying how to go about nurturing the communal life and values of the church *according to their inner logic and imperatives*. It will certainly require discerning more clearly where the gospel of Jesus Christ is most likely to question the larger culture, as well as to celebrate those overlapping places where perhaps the gospel affirms it. And how does this gospel compare and contrast with alternative visions, whether religious, "spiritual," or secular?

This sounds like a recipe that would particularly interest those who value an intellectual understanding of the Christian faith, and so it is; but not exclusively so. While the gospel as understood and served by the church certainly has specific doctrinal content, the gospel is more than ideas or fodder for intellectual rumination. The gospel is the structure that supports worshiping communities, congregations gathered around the risen Lord, a people for whom the gospel is not only a way of thinking, but a way of being—being with God, being with one another, and being with the world outside the church. To nurture our communal life and values according to their inner logic and imperatives requires catechesis (Christian education, Christian formation) as well as a vital liturgy of Word and Sacrament. Catechesis and liturgy become realized and sealed in mission—both in corporate forms of engaging with the world and in commitment to personal discipleship.

Risks and Counterrisks

Enormous obstacles exist, of course—the first being that it seems easiest, and perhaps the most prudent, to keep on doing what we have always done because, even though our numbers have decreased, it doesn't look as though we are going to fade away any time soon. In fact, it is unlikely that Protestant mainline churches are going away in the near future, and probably not ever, because it is rare that religious phenomena of any kind ever die out completely. The greater threat is that the life of mainline Protestant churches will grow ever more bland and indiscriminate, not wanting to risk discouraging anybody who might be willing to hang around with us, for whatever reason.

The purpose of this book is not to engage in a fight to discredit fundamentalism in its various forms. Others have certainly undertaken that. The best way to engage fundamentalism is not by declaring war (highlighting what we are against), but by affirming the substance of classical Christian faith (highlighting what we are for). To square off against fundamentalism by capitulating to the dominant culture of religious skepticism, as though mainline Protestants and the cultural skeptics are natural allies, is surely to misconceive the challenge. And so, this book is intended to point in a another direction: to question both the larger culture and some familiar mainline Protestant adaptations to it, while encouraging commitment to reengaging with classic Christian thought and worship *according to their inner logic and imperatives*. In other words, this book encourages not settling for an identity that is either the antifundamentalist party or the party of the theologically confused, but repositioning ourselves with the help of the rich resources of the catholic tradition, accessed through the catholicity of the Protestant reformers. The reformers' intention, after all, was to reform the catholic faith they had received, not to destroy it or substitute something else for it.

The inner logic and imperatives of orthodox Christianity have everything to do with God, and specifically, the God revealed in Christ by the power of the Holy Spirit—the triune God. God is not just an idea to be tossed around for the pleasure of intellectual speculation and debate, but the "living God," one who moves toward us before ever we spare a thought about ultimate things. The God revealed in Israel and in Christ is a God who acts, who engages with us in ways discernible to the eyes of faith but not necessarily otherwise evident. This is a God about whom we must speak despite the limitations of human language, taking advantage as best we can of the multiple ways that language can be harnessed to point to, suggest, and hint at what is otherwise beyond the capabilities of ordinary discursive speech. Whatever we say will always be partial, inadequate, or easily distorted—particularly whenever one simile or metaphor is isolated, not balanced by others; but God has nevertheless chosen to be revealed to us as living Word, addressed to us in speech and in the person of Christ—a Word we may "hear" and discern by the illumination of the Spirit.

It is time to challenge generic Protestant-think. By "Protestant-think" I intend no disrespect for the intellectual and spiritual traditions that have been deeply nourished by the Reformation. My term describes rather the way that these traditions have been distorted over the generations by their identification with and even merger with the common culture. These distortions mirror and sanctify cultural and religious prejudices that have outlasted the contexts that encouraged them. The church always has to find ways of adapting to local cultures—whether to geographically based cultures or to cultures shaped by the worldviews that dominate particular eras. Once the church has adapted to a culture, it proves to be a challenge to move beyond the adaptation. That is true, I think, for Protestantism in all its varieties, and true in specific ways for each variety, including the so-called mainline. This, then, is the challenge: to shake off the drowsy complacency induced by the comfortable status of having been so very much at home in a culture in which we were held in respect for so long. Staying the course, doing what has become familiar, saying what we usually say is less risky, in some respects, but far riskier in the long run. The issue is whether we have anything to offer authoritatively in a time when the authority that relied on almost universal cultural support for *religion*—defined in America as Christian, and mostly Protestant religion—has run out. And what are the newly established, rarely questioned "authorities" that we ought to question?

Part 1 includes the first two chapters. The first chapter will question the authority of the contemporary cultural consensus that first questioned the older one and has now taken its place, and will consider how over-reliance on Tillich's so-called Protestant principle—a hermeneutic of suspicion—serves to echo and support post-Christian skepticism not only among the secular but also among constituents of the historic mainline Protestant churches. When the habit of questioning is so highly valued that believers are embarrassed by conviction, the balance between questioning and affirmation becomes skewed, making it difficult to sustain a communal identity.

The second chapter suggests grounds upon which to stand while questioning the questioners, and I suggest that that ground is orthodoxy. *Orthodoxy* is a word and a position typically out of favor, whether in secular society or in the Protestant mainstream. Disfavor has come because the word has been associated in secular society with a posture of turning away from anything new in favor of the familiar, no matter what the cost. Protestants dislike the word *orthodoxy* because it has been misappropriated by a narrow spectrum within the larger church. My argument is that classical orthodoxy makes use of a more nuanced understanding of language than is typical of either fundamentalists or their opponents, and so leaves room for paradox. All communities require boundaries, and orthodoxy may serve to define them, generously, while leaving room for diversity. Orthodoxy is less about policing than affirmation, and orthodoxy directs us to the triune God of Scripture and to the ecumenical creeds. It is neither fundamentalism nor a generic spirituality with a Christian tilt.

Moving to part 2, chapter 3 will address a very typical Protestant prejudice against ritual (usually, "ritualism"). The alternative to ritual is novelty and spontaneity. Such "certainties" need to be questioned, particularly as it has become evident that ritual cannot be dismissed simply as empty going-through-the-motions, because ritual is capable of forming worshipers holistically and thus profoundly. In fact, ritual forms worshipers more deeply than does formal instruction, and when shaped by an ecumenical tradition that is older and deeper than the commonplace generic, it protects worshipers from the idiosyncrasies of services cobbled together as though faith and form have nothing to do with each other.

Chapter 4 continues to unfold responses to the question about why it matters what we do on Sunday morning. In many sectors of mainline Protestantism, classical liturgical forms are either unknown, held in suspicion, and/or consulted only piecemeal and intermittently, the dominant value being to design worship locally in a way adapted to the culture of the community. No one can doubt that there are many ways to worship God. Certainly it would be risky to suggest that only one right way exists. Does that mean, then, that there is nothing at stake when the mainstream church assembles to worship on the Lord's Day? I would argue that there is something at stake, and what is at stake is the faith *of the church*. The church is a communion that includes not only the living but also the faithful who have died and also those who are yet to be born. The church includes those present here, and many who are far away. The faith of the church has an integrity that includes the specifics of the pastor's personal faith and our own, but it is not limited to those. What the church does in worship needs to be sufficiently attentive to the faith of the church as a whole that this faith is recognizable as such and liturgically embodied well enough that it can be handed on with confidence. If there is value in affirming an orthodox faith, broadly and generously defined, that faith needs and depends upon an orthodox liturgy.

Chapter 5 considers the importance of what Gordon Lathrop has called "attentiveness to the poor" as an integral part of the church's worship, rooted in a liturgy of Word and Eucharist. Attentiveness to the poor lies near the heart of the church's identity as a "royal priesthood": a communal vocation devoted to intercession and advocacy for the vulnerable, the voiceless, and the neglected. Therefore, attentiveness to the poor has theological and liturgical authority as well as missional implications. What has been called "the Protestant ethic" has often been taken out of its theological and liturgical context, enabling it too frequently to serve as a mask to hide what is really indifference to the poor, if not outright scorn. While mainstream Protestants have not lost their missional impulse to serve others, attentiveness to the poor has frequently lost its intimate association with what we do in the worshiping assembly. In this case, classical liturgical norms inform and critique conventional Protestant thought and practice.

A closing epilogue is followed by a sermon preached on a July 4 weekend, an occasion that always evokes memories of historic challenges to authority.

This book, which is a product of pastoral and teaching experience as well as a few years' experience sitting in a pew, raises questions and makes affirmations, with concern that those Protestants with roots most clearly planted in the Reformation reposition themselves to recover strengths often neglected in what is sometimes a desperate effort to fit in with the dominant culture. Those strengths are rooted in often undervalued historical memory, and have to do with what we teach (our theology), and what we do both in our gathered assemblies and in our communal life expressed as a way of being and acting in the world (liturgy and mission). Conventional Protestant ways of thinking and doing came into being in particular eras and as a result of particular situations. They were intended to serve as remedies for particular problems, but in many cases their shelf life has expired. Thus, this book offers some timely questions that invite a rethinking and suggest a repositioning. The broad ecumenical tradition supplies more than enough rich thought and examples of practice for us to ponder fruitfully. Thus, some affirmations follow.

PART I

1

Question *Which* Authority?

The "Protestant Principle"

IN THE LAST THIRD of the twentieth century, it was commonplace for those living near a university campus to see bumper stickers exhorting the driver in the car behind to "Question Authority." It was hardly an urgent exhortation at the time, or even a brave one, because in the period that witnessed the civil rights movement, the antiwar movement inspired by the Vietnam War, and the rise of feminism, questioning authority was the default setting on campus and far beyond. The exhortation served rather as a kind of encouragement, a rallying cry for all who were joining together to declare independence from the settled consensus in the academy, the state, or the church. Of course, the questioning of authority was hardly new in American society, which was profoundly affected by a Revolutionary War that rebelled against a king; and hardly new even in Western civilization, which, influenced by the Renaissance, Reformation, and the Enlightenment, had granted a high value to critical thinking and questioning received opinion.

The issue of authority is particularly important for Protestants, because Protestantism began as a movement that questioned authoritative positions and practices of the medieval church. Paul Tillich has written of a Protestant principle, which is basically to question anything or anyone that might appear to claim absolute authority. The principle is rooted in the fear of idolatry—of permitting any idea, image, or institution to claim the place of honor that belongs to God alone. This Protestant characteristic has been shaped in large part by the Bible, and particularly shows the influence of the Old Testament prophets, whose calling and gifts were to examine the faith and practice of their own community critically, as from God's point of view. In contemporary times, this principle has acquired such sanctity that it has itself become untouchable.

A secular version of the Protestant principle has been enshrined in the larger culture. Michael S. Roth, president of Wesleyan University, has noted how thoroughly students have digested the idea that being smart means being critical. "The skill at unmasking error, or simple intellectual one-upmanship, is not totally without value, but we should be wary of creating a class of self-satisfied debunkers."[1]

The critical, questioning principle is important and never becomes obsolete, but, like every good thing, it can be swollen out of proportion and become the equivalent of an idol—something beyond question that needs to be questioned. The prophetic tradition in the Old Testament is set, after all, in a larger biblical context of affirmation, and the intention of prophetic questioning is to prune misdirected faith in order that its affirmations be better served. When critical questioning shifts to the point that it becomes the dominant modus operandi of any community, it will distort the life of that community. Some sort of balance needs to be found between questioning and affirming, or even the possibility of communal life will be jeopardized. One can find plenty of unquestioning absolutism in some versions of Protestantism, but a case can be made that for so-called mainline Protestantism—particularly what I would call the mid-American generic kind—affirmation is likely to be greeted with more suspicion than is questioning. The weight given the two is out of balance, not evenly distributed.

Certainly it is and always has been necessary to question authorities, whether openly or by stealth, and will be always. But it is frequently the case that questioning authority eventually leads to a new consensus, one that is itself taken to be authoritative, that might well, in its turn, be questioned. Prudence also requires questioning those who are questioning authority, because questions always come from somewhere, not nowhere, and where the questions come from may well predetermine the answers.

---

1. Ross, "Young Minds in Critical Condition."

Impatient with Doctrine

The poet Christian Wiman, nowhere close to being an authoritarian kind of Christian, has not overstated the case too much when he writes that "churches that go months without mentioning the name of Jesus, much less the dying Christ, have no more spiritual purpose or significance than a local union hall."[2] No doubt Wiman goes a little too far, perhaps underestimating the union hall, but he is certainly right that in nonevangelical, nonfundamentalist American Protestantism of the generic sort, congregations are likely to be impatient with doctrine. A typical pastoral strategy, it seems, is to "demythologize" as much as possible, to maintain a careful distance from even central affirmations of the faith, deferring to the cultural bias toward skepticism in order to avoid disturbing those in the congregation who have already made up their minds that Christian faith is acceptable as long as it is understood as an ethical program. In these circles, the gospel is frequently understood to be of the "teachings of Jesus" variety—"principles to live by"—the sort of angle that has little use for the *person* of Jesus, crucified and risen. Theology is left to the academy, and doctrine is boring, irrelevant, or impossible to understand, but Christianity understood as a moral, therapeutic, or civic program fits the American optimistic temperament. It's about doing good, of course, and what could possibly be wrong with that? The dying Christ, and even more, claims of a risen Christ, just get in the way, don't they? Furthermore, this atheological, nondoctrinal version of Christianity, while in tune with the dominant culture, is likely to understand itself to be heroically challenging a stale and discredited ecclesiastical tradition, thus prophetically questioning authority. This "soft" Protestantism, however, is better understood as the contemporary version of a tradition already well established and that, like any other tradition, needs to be questioned.

In my experience with Presbyterian Church (USA) congregations, most church members seem already to have grasped the fact that the Bible is not always best understood taken literally as though it were a scientific or journalistic account. They understand that language can be used in more than one way. Accordingly, it is no surprise that a biblical text can be understood differently by different readers and communities. Those insights provide a measure of immunity from the influence of authoritarian interpreters relying on a theory of verbal inerrancy. So far, so good. However, it is

---

2. Wiman, *My Bright Abyss*, 138.

easy for the next step to be that since a biblical text can often be interpreted in more than one way, no particular way of understanding the biblical message is more authoritative than any other. All opinions are presumed to be equal. The only Scripture taken to be authoritative is Scripture that affirms what one is already willing to affirm; and we are likely to affirm beliefs and values already in place, values that have already received the endorsement of what Peter Berger has called "the reigning plausibility structure." In other words, it is easy enough to go along with Scripture wherever it does not conflict with what we have been taught by our society to believe since we were first old enough to begin absorbing what "everybody" knows to be true.

What "Everybody" Knows

And what does "everybody" know to be true in the twenty-first century? Except for religious fundamentalists of any sort, "everybody" in the twenty-first century knows that science has all the answers. In fact, everybody is more likely to believe in the omniscience and infallibility of science than most scientists do. Those who know most intimately how the scientific method actually works normally tend to be more modest about the capacities of science to reveal the truth about everything, although there are some striking exceptions in the scientific community. Certainly ever since the fundamentals of Newtonian physics were challenged by quantum theory, what had been taken for absolute truth no longer holds the same level of authority as it did up to and into the last century. Scientists are more likely than others both to know the limitations of science and to be familiar with a long history of one scientific revolution overturning another. We in the general public, however, are more likely to grant authority to what we laypersons take to be science, but what should more accurately be identified as "scientism."

Scientism differs from science in that it makes claims that go beyond the competence of science, much as some fundamentalist Christians make scientific claims that go beyond the competence of theology. Science can describe how things in the material world happen, and, with some limitations, document causes and effects. But science cannot provide an answer to the question of whether there is a God, or whether there is any meaning or purpose in life. True, some scientists have encouraged the lay public to believe that their ability to explain processes is enough to eliminate the possibility that God is, or that life has any particular meaning much less a teleological purpose.

When scientists overstep the bounds of their professional competence, it is not surprising that fundamentalists fight back by discrediting science altogether. Certainly studies of evolutionary processes may suggest that everything that characterizes human life can be explained either by the social and physical environments of our ancestors, or by studies of the biology of the brain, with the implication that if there were really a God, all that is human would have to have come about supernaturally, apart from natural and documentable processes.

To identify processes presumably eliminates the possibility of a God who set those processes in motion and is at work in them. Even when someone claiming scientific authority does not overtly make such claims, the lay public may presume them whenever some new study of early human beings or neurological science is published and makes the news. Scientism, then, is one thing that "everybody" believes in (excepting most of those familiar with the history or philosophy of science), and scientism suggests that all can be explained, and explained more easily without any reference to God. Thus a distorted notion of what science has done and can do has become authoritative for the general public, in spiritual as well as material matters. And, of course, everybody "knows" that there is no other way of knowing anything except by the kind of knowing that comes from the scrupulous use of the scientific method.

"Everybody" knows that globalization means that larger and larger numbers of people are moving from one country to another, from one culture to another, from one context to another. Even in small cities, Christians are likely to encounter people who have been shaped in Hindu, Muslim, Buddhist or other cultures. To the extent that one learns to know something of these neighbors, one discovers that they are normal human beings who are more or less devoted to the plausibility structures into which they have been formed, and able to make an appealing case for them. So it appears that the more we get to know the world with all its complexity and diversity, the clearer it becomes that whatever we have presumed to be spiritually authoritative is just one way among others of interpreting experience.

"Everybody" knows that "spirituality" is only genuine when it is personal, which is to say, individualistic, nondoctrinal, eclectic, noninstitutional, and immune from objective critique. To achieve such spirituality, it is important to avoid commitments—especially to institutions—that might box us in. With the help of novels like Dan Brown's *The Da Vinci Code*, and sensationalized news stories timed for release in Holy Week, "everybody knows" that the church has been engaged in covering up all sorts of truths that, were they to be exposed, would undermine ecclesiastical authority and put orthodox Christianity out of business.

Questioning Which Authority?

How does Christian faith respond to a prevailing cultural environment that is suspicious of authority—particularly of institutions and ways of thinking that have historically been privileged in American society, and, presumably, "ours" to question? How might one question the borrowed authority of a renowned scientist who imagines that possession of academic credentials in a scientific discipline grants authority to make sweeping philosophical proclamations? And, who feels comfortable questioning ideas and beliefs respected in other cultures but new in our own?

One way is simply to say, as used to be said, naively, "It doesn't matter what you believe as long as you're sincere." Few would say that being sincere is the only thing that matters as we form convictions about politics, economics, voting rights; or the curricula for teaching history, social studies, or biology in schools. If sincerity were all that mattered, decision-making about these issues would not produce such tension and conflict. If sincerity were all that mattered, then authority would seem to be centered in each individual, as though each of us created and formed ourselves independently and objectively, immune to any influence beyond ourselves, as though evidence of any external influence would contaminate our natural and essential selves.

It is a fact, of course, that we as individuals are not born in a vacuum, shaping ourselves autonomously, carefully weighing every possible idea or value before absorbing it and committing ourselves to it. We are shaped by communities, beginning with the first community to which we are exposed, which is our family, whatever that family may look like. In subtle ways we digest beliefs and certainties as we are exposed to communities that influence the families in which we are embedded, and then to communities beyond the family circle. If we live in a red state, the statistical likelihood is that we will grow up thinking like a Republican; if we live in a blue state, like a Democrat. If we reach a point of questioning authority, the authority we question will be the authority of our parents first, then the authority of the communities that have touched us in our formative years, or those most clearly indigenous to the dominant culture. We question some authorities, and give others a pass, often guided in our rebellions, great or small, by other communities of influence, peers being but one example. For example, if a community of influence, or a community to which we aspire to belong, praises the virtues of personal distinctiveness, individuality, and suspicion of authority, then we are likely to take the values of that group as authoritative, conforming ourselves to them in such a way as to make ourselves virtually indistinguishable from everybody else in the group.

We are shaped and formed in the interaction between our unique selves and the various environments to which we are exposed, often unconsciously and without any process of self-examination. A mentor of mine who taught history in a major university once lamented that the students who came into his classes in U.S. history tended to leave them with the same prejudices they had brought to class, the only difference being that students left armed with better arguments to support what they had believed in the first place. Of course there were exceptions, but his observation noted the phenomenon that convictions and loyalties are likely to be formed in more complex ways than by simply weighing data objectively.

Some authorities are more likely to be questioned than others. Whatever institutions among us are taken to be established will more likely be examined with a critical eye; those that have recently appeared on the scene and attracted the attention of those fashionably avant-garde are less likely to be critically examined. The exotic will be privileged, while the familiar is viewed with a jaundiced eye.

Authoritative versus Authoritarian

What does this mean for Protestants, and particularly those Protestants most devoted to the Protestant principle, who disdain authoritarianism, but have a hard time distinguishing between being authoritarian and being authoritative? For one thing, it means that we are likely to be embarrassed to be discovered harboring firm religious conviction, as though, in an environment ruled by the reigning plausibility structure, such conviction marks us as conforming, sectarian, fanatic, or unsophisticated. And yet, the firm conviction of unbelievers—the doctrinal certainty that there is no God—is unscientific in its own way, in the sense that it is conviction based on premises that seem self-evident to those who espouse them but cannot be objectively proven to any who are skeptical. Never mind! In our culture, to have a firm religious conviction has been written off as intolerant and, even worse, closed-minded. Yet the atheist or agnostic is likely to be given a pass, at least by the "cultured despisers": those who hold religious faith in disdain. To the extent that Protestants are intimidated by the awesome authority of a cultural consensus that sanctifies questioning authority as long as it is the authority of a church that confesses a faith with doctrinal content, we are at risk of trying to save ourselves from social stigma by minimizing affirmation and maximizing the Protestant principle. Affirmation, then, is crowded out and reduced to those things that are not too likely to be found in conflict with the authority of the prevailing consensus.

When affirmation has to be muted, and it becomes necessary to apologize for conviction or qualify it to the extent that it is scarcely recognizable as conviction, then sustaining a vigorous sense of community becomes very difficult If individual authority always trumps communal authority, then only coincidental similarities of passing tastes and preferences lead to affiliation with one community rather than another. If there is and can be no authoritative voice in matters of faith, it is not surprising that people feel it unnecessary to establish a covenanted relationship with a particular community. Where does this leave much of mainline, mid-American, generic Protestantism? It may sometimes be a safe harbor, a refuge for those fleeing from authoritarian and fundamentalist forms of faith, but it is not the only safe harbor, and there is not much future in just picking up the pieces unless there are some affirmations to be made beyond assurances that our church is theologically open-minded. More commonly, churches that claim theological neutrality find themselves in an uncertain condition, trying desperately to discover an identity that will help them to hang on to their constituencies and whatever public respect remains.

In the twenty-first century, Protestantism appears to be an individualistic movement. Indeed, it has been drifting in that direction for several centuries, but it is not inevitably so, and was not so in its Reformation origins. The reformers of the so-called magisterial Reformation (referring to figures associated with the Lutheran, Reformed, or Anglican reformations) were not individualists, and did not imagine that the church was an open marketplace of opinions, none of which could be authoritatively disqualified, or that the church ought to abandon the faithful to try to think through every issue of faith on their own without any help. In fact, the teachings of the Reformers are more often than not in continuity with one strand or another of theological opinion openly debated by scholars within the medieval church before the Reformation, and the Reformation churches were unequivocally teaching churches. There is at least as much continuity here as discontinuity.

Luther, Calvin, Cranmer, and their allies were committed to worship in Word and Sacrament. Further, the Reformers of the magisterial Reformation affirmed the ancient creeds of the ecumenical church, particularly the so-called Nicene Creed formed in the councils of Nicea, Constantinople, and Chalcedon, and also the Apostles' Creed, a narrative rehearsal of specifically biblical affirmations that originated very early as a baptismal profession of faith. These reformers certainly believed that their teachings were in continuity with the recognized doctors of the undivided church, East and West, and did not hesitate to cite them. The reformers affirmed the need to demonstrate that the reforming church's message was in continuity with apostolic faith. They recognized that even before there was a New Testament, the church had appointed authoritative persons (or groups of persons) to serve as church officers whose responsibility included *episkopē*—oversight.

Defining Landmarks:
Those Things with Which the Church Has to Do

While the Reformers did not consider church councils or church officers to be infallible, and did not claim infallibility for themselves, they affirmed the church's historic recognition that it needed officers whose responsibility included safeguarding the faithful from discredited teaching and teachers. In sum, they understood the Christian faith to be the faith of a community rather than just of an assortment of individuals, and knew from experience that any community with a powerful spiritual message offers openings for exploitation either by those who imagine that their personal vision of the truth trumps that of the community, or by those who see the community as an arena in which to realize their personal ambitions for attention and power. The integrity of the community requires knowledge of the faith that has been handed on—i.e., "traditioned"—from one generation to another, lest the heart of the gospel become lost as innovators with an apparently brand-new insight gather a following and strike out in a direction that may receive popular acclaim even as it leads away from apostolic faith. Think, for one example, of the so-called prosperity gospel, which has made some twenty-first-century preachers hugely successful, measured by society's perception of success.

Christianity is a faith with definition. It has defining landmarks that identify it. Those landmarks include the sacraments, especially baptism and Eucharist (practices both older than the New Testament itself); the Bible—the Old Testament[3] as well as the New—that serves as a distillation of the proclamation and catechesis of the earliest church; and the ecumenical creeds. These exhibit a Christianity rooted in a community of memory and reverence with its anchor in the person of Jesus Christ, an observant Jew who lived, taught, and ministered to all sorts of people in Galilee, Judea, and Samaria; who was crucified under Pontius Pilate; who was resurrected; who ascended to the right hand of the Father; and whose resurrection serves as the promise of a new heaven and earth in God's good time. The landmarks of Christianity also include also the identification of various church officers in every place and every generation who, whether singly or collectively, provide necessary *episkopē*. These landmarks are the things with which we in the church have to do.

By saying that these are the things with which we have to do, I mean that the affirmations of the church in every generation need to be in touch with these defining landmarks. We may add our own confessions of faith, both personal and corporate, to expound on or interpret these landmarks and suggest how they may speak to us now; we may examine each of the landmarks through the lenses of contemporary thought and experience so as to find appropriate ways to affirm them, taking account of new disciplines and discoveries—for example, literary and form criticism, ritual theory, evolutionary theory, or quantum physics. We struggle in every generation to say in our own language and idioms what the Bible and the ecumenical creeds say in the language and idioms of other times and places. We recognize that the church's doctrinal affirmations are often framed to say what the church does not believe as one way of underlining what it does believe but cannot otherwise find adequate language to articulate. In other words, there is a lot of room for continuing reflection, conversation, and debate in and around these basic touchstones, these landmarks with which we have to do as long as we claim to be a Christian church. We can raise all the questions we need to or want to as long as we recognize and respect

---

3. Fleming Rutledge, *And God Spoke*, 2, describes the Old Testament as the "operating system" for the New. In other words, without the Old Testament, the New is nearly incomprehensible, since the New Testament unfolds and develops themes and images from the earlier testament.

these communally honored landmarks as the bases we need to touch as we explore what it means to profess and practice an apostolic faith today.

Some Definitions

Maybe this is the place to define *mainstream* Protestantism. *Mainstream* is different from the frequently used descriptor *mainline*. *Mainline* implies, to my thinking, a position of privilege in society as compared to those bodies not identifiable as mainline. *Mainstream*, on the other hand, implies no special privilege but points to those churches that at least officially embrace the defining landmarks of the Christian faith, as all too briefly described above. For mainstream churches, continuity matters, and so does catholicity.

Although it is hard to define what I mean by mid-American generic Protestantism, most knowledgeable persons know it when they see it. The term *mid-American* is not meant to imply any sort of geography, but rather the characteristic of granting too much authority to the dominant culture; that is, rather too easily conforming to established cultural certainties. A rough generalization might be that a mid-American generic church is inclined to be suspicious of the ecumenical creeds and their affirmations; to be either doctrinally indifferent or narrowly focused on the distinctive views of the denomination, the congregation, or the pastor. The sacraments are either marginalized or minimized, or both—whether by being limited only to occasional celebration or by being flattened out, reduced either to a strictly human exercise of pledging allegiance or to a psychological effort to stir up feelings appropriate to a pivotal event from the past. The larger church, whether the denomination or the ecumenical church, is either ignored or held in suspicion. *Episkopē* from beyond the local community, and sometimes even within it, is likely to be ignored or resented. These churches may project a heavy dose of classical American anti-intellectualism, or they may quite as well think of themselves as more intellectual than everyone else. The poet Christian Wiman, quoted earlier, who found himself drawn to Christian faith as an adult, has little use for those churches that appear to be embarrassed to mention the name of Jesus, much less the risen Christ. They would qualify for categorization as mid-American generic Protestant; but so would another kind of church: the kind that is "infused with the bouncy brand of American optimism one finds in sales pitches"—churches that Wiman describes as "selling shit." Wiman tells it like he sees it, without patience for nuance, but if you take the two together—on the one hand, embarrassment to say too much about Jesus (especially Jesus crucified and risen); and, on the other hand, bouncy optimism typical of consumer culture—you have a reasonably reliable snapshot across a broad spectrum of heavily acculturated mid-American generic Protestantism.

Some congregations that belong to mainstream denominations are more likely to exhibit characteristics of the mid-American generic sort than characteristics that correspond to the official standards of their denomination, so it takes more than reading the name on the outside of the church building to know what you will find inside. And whole denominations are more nearly mid-American generic than anything else. In either case, insofar as they display indifference or hostility to the catholic tradition, they defer to the authority of the broad American cultural consensus that disdains that tradition. Question authority? Yes, indeed! But the authority that cries out to be questioned is precisely that broad American consensus, so visibly incarnated in mid-American generic Protestantism.

Kinds of Authority

Authority is a tricky word. Authority may be identified with institutions and their officers, who possess a certain amount of power to guide and direct those institutions and identify their boundaries. The other kind of authority cannot be defined only by reference to institutional or official power, but it nonetheless exerts the kind of cultural, political, intellectual, or spiritual attraction that draws the allegiance of persons who voluntarily give their consent to it. Religious traditions, particularly those that are old enough to have been tried and tested in many places and times and to have proved adaptable to many cultures, usually possess both kinds of authority—both the institutional and the informal kinds.

At any but a superficial level, authority in matters of faith cannot be established by coercion. Coercion can require one to pretend to honor someone or some institution as authoritative but cannot touch the deepest part of a person. Authority lies within the power of any one of us to grant or to withhold. We may honor as authoritative some individual or body or movement that offers a reasoned and persuasive argument, or offers a convincing testimony, or exhibits characteristics that earn respect and credibility. But it is mistaken to believe that nothing has authority unless it can be proven, and proven even to a skeptic, beyond the shadow of a doubt. To those who love poetry, a poet has authority. To those who love the novel, a novelist may have authority. To those who are moved and uplifted by music or dance, the composer or the lyricist or the dancer has authority. Those who make movies interpret the world from various perspectives, inviting us to see reality through the eyes of artists and insightful observers. The popularity of the arts, whether fine arts or popular arts, suggests the possibility that there may be more than one way to arrive at conviction—more than one way of projecting authority. To the Christian, Jesus speaks with an authority that is persuasive while entirely without coercion, and the gospel of Jesus Christ is, for us, authoritative.

A story in the press reported that fewer families that choose homeschooling for their children are doing so for religious reasons. One homeschooling parent reported that she was providing a curriculum for her children that included an introduction to various world religions, but asserted that she would leave it to her offspring to choose what they wanted to believe. Statistically, the great likelihood is that those children are likely to make the same choice as their parents—that is, indifference. In other words, the views of the parents will prove authoritative for children. Embracing a religious faith is not the same as sorting through ideas, comparing them one with another, and making a logic-driven decision, even if that may happen occasionally. Making a religious commitment more nearly resembles (to use only one imperfect example) falling in love, or, maybe, recognizing a love that seems always to have been there.

Sometimes, of course, personal commitment has been developed from infancy on, as the child has been exposed to the parents' faith and their practice of it, or to their lack of faith and indifference to it. At other times, mature people leave one religious community for another or for none, or experience an adult religious conversion in which they embrace faith for the first time. In all these cases, one can find psychological and sociological reasons to explain a particular person's embrace of faith or rejection of it, or their choice of a faith different from the one in which they were raised. But being able to offer explanations for the processes of embracing or rejecting faith does not make faith invalid—as though, when it comes to faith, people should have to leave behind their identity as psychosocial, flesh-and-blood human beings. From the Christian point of view, faith is a gift of God, however it occurs, even though acquiring it can be described, even if not exhaustively, in terms of human processes. When the seed of faith begins to flower, the object of faith is granted authority in the life of the person who embraces it.

I was raised by parents who belonged to a church but kept their distance from it. When I was a teenager, a friend who was a devoted Roman Catholic began to try to convert me to the tradition he had learned so well in church and parochial school. I loved our debates but was working with very little information, so I sought out books that would provide some material to support my resistance. It occurred to me that maybe my trump card might be the New Testament itself, so I began to read it, at least a chapter every day. My purpose was not to become devout but to gather ammunition to lob in his direction. By the time I reached the last chapter of the book of Revelation, having read the entire New Testament through, I discovered that something had changed. Without being able to identify a moment when the change occurred or even how it had occurred, I had begun to read as one to whom this message was addressed rather than as one who was merely accumulating information. I read as one within the circle of the faith rather than as one who stood outside it. The Christian faith, as I had been introduced to it in the New Testament, had become authoritative for me.

Of course, I still had questions, some of which were answerable and have been answered over time, and others that have required pondering over a lifetime without any certainty that a definitive answer will emerge in the years that remain to me—or ever on this side of eternity. However, faith comes first, and then follows the reasoning that finds support for it. Faith is quite rational—certainly as reasonable as anything else—but it is not ordinarily the product of a pure reasoning process. As one proceeds in the life of faith, one takes the claims that faith makes, working them out in the context of one's ever-widening personal experience and the universe of secular knowledge.

The Church as Mother and Mentor

But one does not work out these claims all alone. Augustine and the reformer John Calvin and probably others have described the church, metaphorically, as a mother who nurtures her children. Another image of the church may be as a mentor, coaching those who seek faith and formation in the practice of that faith. Because I have found authoritative the gospel of the triune God to whom the church and its Scripture testify, I have trusted the church to tutor me in that faith. After all, where one finds substantial nourishment, one is likely to return, again and again.

Trust, of course, is a risky business, and it is risky even to recommend it when a characteristic of our era is to mistrust institutions, whether political or religious. Mistrust of institutions is particularly prominent among Protestants, for whom individual authority tends to trump communal norms. Certainly history records examples of misuse of authority by the corporate church, but even recent history offers examples of individuals who, claiming personal authority of one kind or another, are far from trustworthy in matters of faith. One example is Warren Jeffs, leader of the Fundamentalist Church of Jesus Christ of Latter-Day Saints, convicted in 2011 of child sexual abuse; or Jim Jones of the notorious People's Temple. Or one might think of the leaders of various white power "Christian identity" cults. Prudence forbids mentioning a number of contemporaries who, though far less extreme, seem to fit the category of religious entrepreneur, apparently ignorant of, indifferent to, or hostile to the broad catholic tradition.

The ecumenical church, it seems to me, with its various safeguards in place, proves more reliable on the whole, though not infallible. And so it is to the church to which I turn to tutor me in the faith. Not to a single denomination only, but to the greater church, and particularly those parts of it that may be identified as respectful of the historic and defining landmarks that keep us rooted in what we call, for lack of a better name, apostolic faith. In that sense, the church, whose work is to build us up in faith, is authoritative. Not because of some theory of ecclesiastical infallibility, but because its nurture has evoked in me a trusting response. Because I trust the authority of the church—sometimes exhibited in and through its pastors and teachers, and sometimes in spite of them—I feel comfortable exploring my questions within the circle of that worshiping community's thought and practice.

Of course, as one who finds the worship of the church to be vitally important for my own spiritual well-being, I fully understand my friend and colleague who laments that though he's a Christian on Sunday, by Thursday he's on the verge of being an atheist. Hyperbole, of course, but it represents the truth that it is possible to be a believer and a doubter at the same time and by spells. Faith requires the continuing support and nurture of the faithful community. Surely, some days, I question everything I have ever imagined that I could know for certain. It is not wrong to question, including to question authority.

But where does one stand when questioning authority? In Britain, the party out of power sometimes describes itself as "Her Majesty's loyal opposition." One may question from a standpoint of *loyal* opposition, or from a place simply of opposition. One may question from within the circle, or from without. Within the communion of the church, one may be deeply loyal to the identifying landmarks and nevertheless find ample room for exploration in them and around them, using one's questions to probe more deeply into the Christian faith and investigate the ways it either coheres with or clashes with the common culture as well as with alternative worldviews. Finding myself without prior intention within the communal circle that finds the church's testimony both winsome and persuasive, catholic Christianity (experienced through a reforming lens) is authoritative. Therefore, my commitment causes me to question other authorities, and particularly the authority of a typically overconfident North American cultural consensus.

As one who has been shaped and influenced by that consensus as much as anyone else, I need no permission to question it. The American culture has been deeply marked by egalitarianism, a quality that I admire and that influences the way I vote. But insofar as the premise that all human beings are created equal seems to lead to the sloppy conclusion that all ideas, opinions, and values are equal, or that respect for others requires treating every person's idea, opinion, or value as though all were equal, I beg to differ. Some voices speak with more authority than others. There is Stalin, on the one hand, whose proletarian ideology led to the Gulags, and, on the other hand, there is Mandela, whose egalitarian agenda led to national reconciliation. Not equal. Few thoughtful people in our culture would disagree. We all make necessary judgments every day about ideas, opinions, and values circulating in the culture. Yet, masquerading as a kind of broad-minded tolerance, a consensus seems to have formed that *religious* ideas, opinions, and values are all equal. Perhaps all are equally right, when you get right down to it, or all equally wrong, or all unimportant in any case, or all simply an equally unconstructive nuisance, a source of oppression we need to get rid of.

Granted, to affirm one of these various perspectives and conclusions—all are equally good or all equally bad—is, in itself, to make a claim that one of those positions or the other is right while any other is wrong, which is not, I think, different from taking a doctrinal stance—in this case, one framed as a sweeping generalization. But any of these indiscriminate generalizations lead to the same end. They relegate religious faith of whatever sort and from any source to something without authority: to something that doesn't matter much unless it annoys us, to something to take or leave, depending on our disposition.

The bottom line would seem to be that since each person makes an individual decision about what to believe and where to lodge one's allegiance, the only authority lies with individuals. According to this view, there is no role for communal authority. Further, since the individual is understood, in popular culture at least, to be virtually self-made, everyone has equal standing whatever their level of acquaintance with the issues. Everyone votes, don't they? Even when they know nothing of a candidate beyond the television ads? Likewise, nobody needs a church to mentor them in faith, do they? To "tell me what to think"? After all, it is possible to form opinions about religious matters even if one's knowledge about them is based only on occasional exposure to a Sunday school class as a child, or on a radio preacher, or on a social studies unit, or on rare visits to a church service for which one was entirely unprepared, not recognizing before, during, or after it that any preparation might be necessary.

Even a great many people who share this cultural consensus—it's all a matter of opinion, and all opinions are equal—are, in fact, members of churches, and some become teachers and church officers and active members of decision-making bodies. So it is not too surprising that across a wide swath of even mainstream Protestantism, one finds deep suspicion of religious claims to authority, especially when these claims diverge from the common culture. Somehow, in American society ever since King George III, whoever affirms authority is more likely to find herself on the defensive than is the dissenter. Nowhere has distaste for authority been more evident than in the fracturing of American Protestantism.

Is There Too Much "Protest" in Protestantism?

When Reformation Day comes around every year on the Sunday nearest October 31, I find myself uncomfortable. It's not that I mind celebrating the contributions of reformers such as Martin Luther and John Calvin, or Bucer and Cranmer and Knox and many others, or even, generations later, John Wesley. My discomfort stems from the sense that it is all too easy for us Protestants to imagine that dissent and protest against communal authority is a norm for living out our Christian life in the church. In the sixteenth century, dissent and protest proved necessary but sometimes took extreme forms; and, in any case, the papal church did not handle dissent and protest well. The Reformation introduced necessary reforms, but at the cost of a rupture in the body of Christ. Even if we can make our peace with that, it is more difficult to make our peace with the fact that Protestants have taken protest and schism to be a model for handling differences when they arise, whether with respect to theological debates, ecclesiastical policy, or the distribution of power. The result has been to make it easy for someone with a passion about a single issue to turn the rise of this passion into an occasion for separating the faithful from the unfaithful—where faithfulness is measured with respect to that one inflamed, existentially urgent, issue.

But where is the spiritual sensitivity that recognizes that dividing the church has negative spiritual consequences of enormous proportions? Counting the number of separate denominational bodies, not to mention the independent congregations, is staggeringly difficult and altogether embarrassing. The usual perception is that the line of division in a denominational split will be drawn between so-called conservatives and liberals, although the choice of those labels often overlooks some subtleties. The likely result is that when the conservatives have it all to themselves, no longer troubled by the questions and concerns of the liberals, they are inclined to become more ingrown and sectarian; while the liberals, having shed the conservatives, lose their ballast, and tend to be more easily swayed by the cultural winds. Further, as dissenters break away from the dissenters of another generation, and then their descendants repeat the process, it becomes easier and easier to wander further and further from the landmarks that serve to identify the faith of the church. The so-called Protestant principle serves a purpose, but it needs to be balanced by equally vigorous affirmation of those landmarks that have served to anchor the ecumenical church in apostolic faith.

Those Protestant churches that have managed to maintain some sort of respect for the landmarks, the touchstones that mark classical Christian faith, have reached the right historical moment for letting go of some of the less helpful convictions we have held on to so tightly. One of those is the popular perception that the Reformation was basically a do-over in which we started all over again, this time getting Christianity right. (A corollary of that in a fractured and fracturing church is that whenever our particular group broke away from its predecessor, we imagine that we have started all over again and have finally got it right.)

No doubt the pre-Reformation church got some things wrong and needed reform, just as the post-Reformation churches have and do. But no church that claims a specifically Christian identity can seriously imagine that centuries of Christian history, thought, piety, devotion, and reflection can simply be canceled or written off because the church took a wrong turn here or there; no self-identifying Christian church can seriously imagine that it is really possible to start over from scratch. Even when the do-over appeals to the Bible, the inescapable fact remains that the New Testament canon was not generally recognized as such until the late fourth century CE. This is the same broad period that saw the convening of the ecumenical councils that formulated the Nicene Creed. The church's recognition of the canon of Scripture, which made it a touchstone, an identifying landmark of the Christian faith, was the culmination of a long process of informal reception by the church—the same church that affirmed the doctrine of the Nicene Creed as being in continuity with the tradition that had both produced and affirmed the canon.

Authority and Community

Bible and Creed come from the same worshiping community that had gathered around Word and Sacraments even before the writing of the first book of what came to be called the New Testament. The magisterial Reformation, however critical reformers may have been of medieval elaborations and digressions, nevertheless honored the communal tradition from which stemmed both Bible and Creed, not imagining themselves to be sweeping out the distinguishing landmarks and starting the church all over again. Their mainstream heirs get it too (at least, officially). In practice, however, it is unfortunately all too often the case that we don't get it, as though the present moment is all that matters; as though our predecessors in the community of faith have nothing useful to say to us and, indeed, may as well be, for all practical purposes, excommunicated. A culture that has been shaped by the ideas that progress is inevitable and that progress means leaving the past behind is vulnerable to becoming indifferent, if not hostile, to history. Any who doubt it may reflect on the fact that old heresies continue to spring up generation after generation, each time winning adherents who imagine they are encountering a fresh new idea. While we are questioning authority, we might begin by questioning the authority of that skeptical frame of mind that either scorns or ignores those who have taught and nurtured our community in some of the most dynamic moments in its history; and we might be skeptical of that frame of mind that turns receptively and with far less scrutiny to worn ideas that pass as new.

It is never safe to surrender the prerogative of questioning authority, whether specific persons in authority or authoritative cultures, whether secular, political, "spiritual," or religious authorities. At the same time, it is not possible to live fruitfully in community without being willing to risk a measure of trust, including trusting persons who hold responsible offices, and trusting communities. Trusting is not the same as ruling out any possibility of questioning; trust does not grant to any person, community, or culture infallible status or immunity from criticism. But whenever there exists a perpetual state of suspicion, communities suffer from polarization and conflict, a condition abundantly apparent in twenty-first-century U.S. political culture. At the point of cultivating trust and discerning trustworthiness the historic Protestant mainstream needs to begin treating its overreliance on the Protestant principle.

I trust the broad catholic and reforming tradition and believe that it speaks in diverse voices that nevertheless prove to be collectively authoritative and that therefore deserve to be taken seriously. To honor that tradition is not to say that I am very confident in the leadership and structure of the Roman Catholic Church (which certainly does not have exclusive claim to the word *catholic*) or in the very public positions it takes on many contemporary social issues, although Pope Francis, with his concern for the poor and marginalized, is certainly an appealing figure. Yet my level of trust in mid-American generic Protestantism is very low, in large part because of its indifference to the spiritual and intellectual treasures of the ecumenical, catholic tradition, including the representation of this tradition in the Reformation. Those Protestants who set themselves as opponents of science and aim to use political power to return to an idealized past, striking out against all contemporary thought, deserve a vote of no confidence. Any religious community that espouses hatred or violence, or that claims special privilege in God's name at the expense of others, contributes to the rising hostility to faith of any name and any kind, and certainly forfeits the respect of thoughtful people. It is no wonder, in today's environment, in which the headlines go to the fanatical—whether Christian or Muslim or Jewish or Buddhist or something else—that even educated people in North America are rarely acquainted with the fact that these traditions hand on, to those who will receive them, treasures from other generations—treasures that are still able to engage the intellect and capture the heart. So, while prizing specifically Protestant contributions to the ongoing development of a truly catholic tradition, let us question the questioners and ponder the possibility that the great treasure of the church is—can it be?—orthodoxy.

2

What's the Matter with Orthodoxy?

Orthodoxy: Playing Defense?

WE MAINSTREAM PROTESTANTS NEED to reposition ourselves in relation to the word *orthodox*. Admittedly, orthodoxy has a bad reputation. In secular circles, *orthodoxy* equates with old-fashioned, rigid, stale, unimaginative—yesterday's news. It stands as a negative contrast to that which is fresh, au courant, and boundary breaking. Almost no one welcomes being described as orthodox, which might just be the kiss of death in some circles. To be orthodox is to be viewed with a jaundiced eye, not only by the religiously indifferent, but also by many mainstream Christians, perhaps especially because the designation *orthodox* is one that a narrow slice of evangelical Protestantism has claimed for itself.

Among Protestants, *orthodox* became a bad word in the wake of the early twentieth century fundamentalist-modernist controversy centered on biblical authority. Those who were repelled by so-called higher criticism—new ways of studying the Bible—established a list of five "fundamentals" identified as essential to orthodox Christianity. They were:

- biblical inspiration and the inerrancy of Scripture
- the virgin birth
- belief that Christ's death was the atonement for sin
- the bodily resurrection of Jesus
- the historical reality of the miracles of Jesus

The motive in identifying these "fundamentals" was to secure the faith and preserve it from any approach that threatened to undermine it. However, in the process of shoring up their defenses, the fundamentalists nailed down and froze in place one way of understanding biblical affirmations that are capable of being understood in more than one way and, arguably, understood more faithfully when not boxed in so rigidly. All five affirmations have a place in the historic tradition of ecumenical Christianity, but by choosing to interpret these five affirmations from a defensive posture, their defenders overlooked the fact that the affirmations had not always been understood in the same way. The fundamentalists placed, in fact, a twentieth-century rationalist spin on doctrines that had been taken seriously in more nuanced ways by Christian thinkers past and present who were unquestionably orthodox.

Taking the Bible seriously does not require a fundamentalist reading of it. The church has always believed in biblical inspiration, which is to say that the Holy Spirit was at work in the formation of the Bible but also, and necessarily, at work in both the communal and individual processes of transmitting and receiving it; as well as in the work of hearing, reading, understanding, and "inwardly digesting" it, to borrow a phrase from the Book of Common Prayer. Inerrancy? Wherever human language is concerned, there is the capacity for error, whether in language expressed or language received. A doctrine of inerrancy is no doubt intended to reinforce and support the authority of the Bible; and yet Scripture's authority is not autonomous but derivative. We don't start out as agnostics in matters of faith who nevertheless hold an a priori belief that the Bible is authoritative. Faith in the God of the Bible and respect for its testimony go together. Better to say, I think, that insofar as the Bible exhibits God's character and disposition towards us in Jesus Christ, it is reliable, and we can count on it as a primary vehicle by which God reaches out to us in grace and directs the church as it endeavors to keep the apostolic faith and hand it on.

Is the doctrine of the virgin birth about biology or theology? If the church were to say as much about it as did the Apostle Paul or the Gospel of Mark or John, we would say nothing. As for biology, we would do best to keep a modest agnosticism. Theologically, the doctrine is one way of affirming that Jesus Christ is not an accident of history or an example of heroic spiritual striving but comes to us out of the very intention and purpose of God.

The church's Bible affirms the atonement in the sense that in Christ, God has freed us from what in Hinduism might be called the law of karma.

In other words, we will not reap precisely what we have sown. As sinners, we sow all sorts of mischief and ugly things along with much that is worthy; Christ has freed us from the fear that God is required, consequently, to even the score. One biblical image of atonement is that of God, in Christ, generously paying off a debt in our behalf. Of course, every relationship costs something to those who want to be in relation, and so the metaphor of paying off a debt works as long as it is not pushed too far. God's paying a debt on our behalf is one among several atonement metaphors in the New Testament. All the atonement metaphors serve the purpose of affirming that God absorbs the cost of a relationship with us—a cost that is certainly beyond our human capability. It's better to understand the atonement in terms of relationship rather than in terms suitable to the courtroom. *Substitutionary* atonement is an example of courtroom language, implying that God has done an end run around God's own rules.

The faith of the church is that Christ is risen from the dead. The use of the word *bodily* is accurate, to a point, but it says either too much or too little if it is the only modifier to describe the risen Christ. It would be wise to remember that the Jesus who appeared to his remaining disciples on two consecutive Sunday evenings (John 20) was able to join them in a room with locked doors but in a tangible body whose wounds the disciples could see and touch. The paradoxical conclusion must be that the risen Christ was neither a resuscitated corpse nor a ghost. His resurrection body was in recognizable continuity with the body of the mortal Jesus—not identical with it, but clearly a transformed version of it.

The miracle stories of Jesus healing the sick and broken, exorcising the afflicted, and raising the dead are integral to the Christian gospel. They testify to Jesus as the finger of God, as the inauguration of God's messianic reign (kingdom). When fully manifest, the reign of God will be the point where all will be made whole in body and mind, and we will be freed from evil influences that undermine us physically, emotionally, and spiritually. Finally we will be freed from the fear of death.

Are all the biblical accounts meant to be understood as journalistic snapshots of unambiguous supernatural events, or is it possible that some use a simple and accessible story as a way of making a theological affirmation? (John Calvin, after all, spoke of the Scripture as God's baby talk.[1]) For

---

1. McNeill, ed., *Calvin: Institutes* 1.13.1., 121: "For who even of slight intelligence does not understand that, as nurses commonly do with infants, God is wont in a measure to 'lisp' in speaking to us?"

example, the story of Jesus calming the sea would seem to be less a description of a historical event and more a theological statement about Jesus's identity: the story links him with the Lord to whom Psalm 107:24 testifies, since in the Old Testament it is Yahweh who overcomes chaos. "He made the storm be still, and the waves of the sea were hushed" (107:29).

The Uses of Language

Ever since the controversies of the early twentieth century, it has been fundamentalists who have been identified as conservative, even though their particular concerns do not conserve many things that classical Christianity has judged to be of equal or greater importance; and their interpretation even of these "fundamentals" would not always square with some of the interpretations of the doctors of the church and of the Protestant reformers. Being on the defensive is not identical with being conservative. The question, as always, is, what are we trying to conserve? Those with a broader vision of the heritage of the church catholic have a more persuasive claim to being those who conserve the great treasures of the faith, but the adjective conservative has, nevertheless, been surrendered to those with narrower interests, who have similarly laid claim to be exclusively entitled to the orthodox identity. In the process, both adjectives have suffered the fate of being associated with that which is regressive, defensive, and unimaginative. Orthodoxy, however, should not be understood to be either antithetical to or identical with *liberal, conservative,* or *progressive*—as though orthodoxy must be only one of these things and not another, especially apart from any consideration of context.

An observer looking over a shoulder at the fundamentalist-modernist controversy might conclude that the so-called progressives were as likely as the fundamentalists to insist on their own version of literalism. Was Jesus resurrected "bodily"? If "bodily" cannot be understood in any other way than the literal resuscitation of a corpse, then those who find that definition unacceptable may see no option but simply to deny it; or they may propose their own specificity, which might be whatever is the opposite of "bodily": perhaps "spiritually," whatever that may mean, or "psychologically," or "symbolically." Again, that is to say too little or too much. One may gather the impression that there is no alternative but a simple binary solution—i.e., either "bodily" or not-bodily. And yet, there are alternatives to the simple B or not-B, if one is willing to consider affirmations that make use of paradox.

After all, all human language is symbolic. When language has to do with things that we cannot see, count, or touch, it requires us to extrapolate from language that communicates by way of its association with ordinary mundane things. Language always requires us to use our imaginations. Since our imaginations tend to be limited, it is easy to treat language about holy things as though it is no different from the language used in the manual that tells how to assemble the tricycle bought for a child at Christmas. In other words, we are inclined to shrink the language, to limit it prematurely. This shrinking either results in some sort of fundamentalism that closes down the roominess of the biblical language and images, or it leads to skepticism, which, similarly, narrows the language and images, as though they could be understood in only one way. Thus, fundamentalism and skepticism both crowd out whatever overflows the limits of ordinary discourse and so invites us to stretch our imaginations. The poet knows the suppleness of language, and so does the lover of literature. Language makes use of subtlety, nuance, and paradox, especially when dealing with holy things. As I have written elsewhere, "Biblical language and images tend to be large, and they have within them a lot of room to stretch. This is why one has to live with them, not merely look them up in a dictionary."[2] This can be true of theological language and is certainly true of liturgical language.

For example, the Nicene-Constantinopolitan Creed affirms that Jesus Christ was both God and human.[3] The Council of Chalcedon adopted a formula to interpret the relationship between Jesus's deity and his humanity. It reads, in part, that Jesus Christ is "perfect both in deity and also in human-ness; this self-same one is also actually God and actually man . . . He is of the same reality as the Father as far as his deity is concerned and of the same reality as we are ourselves as far as his human-ness is concerned."[4] If this is confusing, it is because it is, to say the least, an extraordinary use of language. How can Jesus be both God and human? Perhaps it might be possible to imagine a hybrid identity—partly God and partly human—but the language of the Chalcedonian formula is as explicit as it is precisely in order to rule out the suggestion that Jesus is half God and half human (or, to put it another way, neither fully God nor fully human). Since no precedents

---

2. Byars, *What Language*, 7.

3. In the Nicene Creed: "God from God, true God from true God, begotten, not made, of one Being with the Father . . . For us and for our salvation he came down from heaven . . . and became truly human."

4. Leith, *Creeds*, 35–36, as cited in Johnson, *Praying and Believing*, 89.

in human experience provide adequate language to make this affirmation that Jesus is both fully God and fully human, the doctors of the councils had to innovate, to use language not strictly logical but nevertheless supple, in order to make its point—a point that needs to be grasped intuitively as much as reasoned. Paradox.

Defining *Orthodox*

So, what about the word *orthodox*? Technically, it derives from two Greek words—*ortho* and *dokeo*—meaning "right thinking or teaching." It is the responsibility of the church, and the specific responsibility of church officers, to hand on the faith in such a way as to maintain the integrity of its message. This includes respecting the rich tradition of reflection and teaching that proceeds historically from the defining landmarks (see chapter 1), and that invites continuing conversation rooted in and respectful of those landmarks, rather than in ignorance, indifference, or defiance of them. This conversation broadens and becomes richer whenever it includes the voices of those social, ethnic, or gender groups who heretofore have not been invited to the table.

The Christian faith, like the Jewish faith, is a communal affair, not a strictly private doctrine or a private piety. We are accountable to one another, and particularly so as we ponder the precious things that we received from our forebears in the faith, and that the greater part of the church, Catholic and Protestant, has held in common. It is reasonable that a community ought to be able to consider some matters to be settled. I don't mean that settled matters may never again be closely examined or viewed through fresh eyes; nevertheless, within the faith they need to be respected as set firmly in place. It would not be profitable to reconsider, for example, whether the canonical Bible ought to be edited—say, in the manner of Thomas Jefferson's radical revision of the New Testament—or whether some books should be removed or others (ancient or modern) added.[5] To do any of those things in a worldwide ecumenical church that shares, for the most part, a common Scripture would invite chaos. In this hypothetical scenario, any group or any number of groups might re-create its own Bible to support specific interests. Likewise, the ecumenical creeds are no longer open for negotiation. The Nicene Creed has served as an anchor for centuries as the church continues to ponder the mystery of Christ as the

5. McDonald, *Formation of the Bible*.

incarnate Second Person of the Trinity. To discard it, or edit it, imagining that we could reintroduce the questions to which it responds as though it were possible to start the conversation all over again (in the absence of the earliest participants) is a recipe for disaster. Reopening the questions addressed by the Nicene Creed would create a veritable Tower of Babel of theological debate, and would certainly deal a lethal blow to what remains of the catholicity of the church. As Margaret Bendroth points out,

> a conversation is not a verbal free-for-all, where anyone can come in and shift the subject to something completely different . . . A truly creative conversation builds on what has been said before, exploring nuances and suggesting different interpretations—but never assuming that the people who began it have nothing more to say and can be safely ignored. The living do not own the conversation any more than those past or those yet to come.[6]

The church long ago reached a consensus that Marcionism, Docetism, and Pelagianism, for example, were not in accord with the faith that it had received and that has been embodied in its worship, even though these and other heresies keep resurfacing under other names. It is unfruitful, to say the least, to imagine that every issue, every debate that has taken place over more than two millennia, needs to be reopened in every generation.

Granted, the canonical Scriptures and the ecumenical creeds have human fingerprints all over them, but how otherwise could it be? The alternative would be Scriptures and creeds supernaturally given without being touched by human cultures, politics, questions, passions, or interests. Were that the case, neither Bible nor creeds could possibly be accessible to mortals, much less means of grace.

> The bishops who composed the original [Nicene] creed in 325 were intensely aware that they were crafting the first ecumenical or churchwide statement of its kind. To ensure broad acceptance of their work, they drew extensively on the format and wording of regional creeds of undisputed antiquity and authority . . . including the creed used by Christians in Palestine.[7]

The defining landmarks—worship in Word and sacrament, the Bible, the ecumenical creeds, and *episkopē* do not come with guarantees, but they have mapped out the boundaries within which a continuing conversation

---

6. Bendroth, *Spiritual Practice*, 94–95.
7. Soulen, *Divine Name(s)*, 39, 41.

among the faithful takes place. These foundational landmarks are not dispensable, and, for orthodox Christians, must be honored as firmly emplaced. These are the things with which we have to do.

Does an affirmation of orthodoxy tie God down? Put God in a box? Deny the freedom of the Holy One to move in ways we do not expect, to speak in accents we do not recognize, to judge what we cherish, or to cherish what we have judged? The moment we dare to utter a single word about God and God's ways, orthodox or heterodox, simple or complex, we run that risk. The alternative would seem to be to say nothing, but that option has been closed to those who cannot turn away from what they have discerned in the voice, heart, and person of Jesus Christ. We must say something, even though to speak is risky, but the risk is shared when we link arms with the faithful of many generations who have questioned, reflected, worshiped, and struggled to frame affirmations together, rooted in the encounter with God in Christ.

Those who for reasons of conscience cannot acknowledge or respect the landmarks that identify orthodox Christianity are, of course, free to depart from it or to create variations on it, in ways minor or major, as many have already done—right up to and beyond Mary Baker Eddy and Joseph Smith. Nevertheless, those who identify as orthodox have no reason to apologize or be embarrassed, as though they lack the intellectual resources to imagine an entirely different way that Christianity might have developed, or the chutzpah to strike out on their own in a new direction.

Orthodoxy and Diversity

Protestant churches rooted in the magisterial Reformation of the sixteenth century and also some that derive from them are, as far as their official standards attest, orthodox in the senses I have described. They share orthodoxy with the Roman Catholic Church and the Orthodox churches of the East. The label *orthodox* does not imply unanimous agreement in doctrine or ecclesiastical polity, much less unanimity on moral and ethical issues such as those so frequently debated these days having to do with reproduction and human sexuality. The label *orthodox* points rather to the fact that these churches all stand in a tradition based upon and respectful of certain defining landmarks, even when the churches approach them differently. Not all who might accurately be described as orthodox value diversity, or value it in the same way, but orthodoxy is at its heart nevertheless at least tolerant of diversity, although such tolerance is exhibited in varying degrees by the several churches that lay claim to being described as orthodox. That a measure of diversity is not incompatible with orthodoxy is evident by the fact that the New Testament itself has not just one but four canonical Gospels, each *according to* a different evangelist. Each of the four proceeds according to its own interests and perspective, usually coming out of and intended for specific communities at particular times and places. Each canonical gospel is organized differently, and their narrative lines are not identical, but they have enough in common that they function more or less as different dialects of the same mother tongue. It is not that only one is entitled to be authoritative whereas the other three are judged to be heterodox. The four, with their diversity, their very fourness, are equally the heritage of the ecumenical church.

The boundaries of the faith are wider than some of the various constituent parts of the church may imagine, and yet there are boundaries. Of necessity, every community, including the ecumenical church, needs boundaries. Is Jesus Christ only a human being? Or is he God in disguise, only appearing to be human? Or is he a second deity alongside the God known in Israel? Is Mary Baker Eddy right that the entire created world is simply the product of an unhealthy and distorted human imagination? Is Joseph Smith right that Father, Son, and Holy Spirit are three entirely separate divine beings? Beliefs have consequences, and for that reason it is not possible that any and every belief can simply be welcomed within the tent as though respect for diversity requires no discrimination between one doctrine and another. The history of the church records serious theological debates that include examining the trajectory of doctrines to see where they ultimately lead. For example, if Jesus is judged to be a human being only, or even if he were to be judged a divine being but not the incarnation of Israel's God, then to honor him as Sovereign (Lord) in our worship and our professions of faith would be idolatrous and blasphemous. If Jesus is a divine being only masquerading as human, then his death on the cross is a deception. If the visible world is only a figment of the human imagination, then the created, material world is devalued—including our bodily lives.

When doctrinal debates become passionate, it is frequently the case, if not always, that big things are at stake. The purpose of sustained theological reflection and debate is to explore deeply enough to uncover the implications of affirming one doctrine rather than another. When the issues become clear enough to draw a consensus, the result is the clarification of boundaries. Incarnation is a doctrine that the church affirms and is obligated to teach, even though it stretches the imagination. Reincarnation, on the other hand, is not.

Are Boundaries Necessary?

Most creeds—certainly including the Nicene—have been produced in response to one crisis or another, either within the church or in relation to the larger culture. The Theological Declaration of Barmen responded to National Socialism's attempts to tame and silence the German church. The South African Belhar Confession rebuked the doctrine of apartheid that had been all too easily blessed by the church on behalf of the host culture. Much earlier, the Nicene Creed answered the need to define terms—to identify who Jesus Christ is and how he relates to God—in a time when an opening had occurred for the church to expand its mission dramatically. Creeds and confessions set boundaries, but not arbitrarily. The process used by the doctors of the councils of Nicea and Chalcedon included both a careful reading of Scripture and a respectful attentiveness to the faith of the church as they had received it; and they framed their consensus in the most sophisticated language available at the time.

Boundaries matter. They ought not to be drawn too narrowly, nor should they be drawn so broadly that discerning the essential character of the community and what it means to belong to it becomes impossible. The history of the church makes it clear enough that in every generation and in many places there have been and will continue to be theological, doctrinal, and ethical land mines that need to be discerned, identified, and avoided. The identification of boundaries requires church officers whose responsibilities include enabling an authoritative teaching ministry of the church and exercising appropriate *episkopē*.

In the period when the New Testament was being written, *episkopē* (oversight) was exercised first by individual apostles, then by groups of *presbyters*, then by bishops (*episkopoi*) who were pastors of the church in a particular place, perhaps "in council" (i.e., assisted by other officers). (It is wise, of course, to presume diversity and overlap in the earliest church rather than to presume a simple linear development.) In time, however, pastor-bishops became responsible for oversight of larger communities extended over wide geographical areas. The Reformation introduced variations on *episkopē*, including presbyterial and synodical forms of collective oversight as well as bishops.

Originally, at least, and ideally, those exercising *episkopē* were (and still ought to be) officers who exercise pastoral ministries that keep them closely in touch with the whole spectrum of the faithful in their charge. While it is cause for shame that various officers, individual and collective, who are responsible for *episkopē* do not always recognize each other's authority, it is nevertheless worth noting that the various bodies charged with *episkopē* are not entirely ignorant of or indifferent to each other's ministries, and even show themselves capable of learning from each other. For example, the several interconfessional dialogues (Anglican–Roman Catholic, Reformed–Orthodox, and the like) are understood not as interfaith encounters but as intrafaith conversations among representatives of groups that share the defining landmarks that enable participants to speak the same language, though with different accents.

Contemporary culture in both Europe and North America is suspicious of boundaries. It prizes the quality of inclusiveness to the extent that any drawing of boundaries is all too easily denounced as exclusiveness. The irony is that in the various formal and informal communities of secular society, inclusiveness is not treated as an absolute value—one that requires the dismantling of all boundaries. Political parties have identifying characteristics distinctive enough to draw participants to choose one party rather than another. Groups that exist to strengthen laws against drunk driving, groups that support or oppose gun control, or groups that provide mutual support for those fighting alcoholism or drug abuse are all built around identifying principles—doctrinal standards, if you will—that form communities.

Why, then, does mainstream Protestantism appear to be so defensive about affirming an identity that, similarly, is bound to result in leaving some folks out, even though without malice? The very word *catholic*, part of the Apostles' Creed, means "universal," and refers to a church meant to welcome those of every race, ethnicity, nationality, and class, leaving room for those who struggle and question. But certainly to be catholic does not mean embracing as equally worthy every religious impulse or theological opinion. Mainstream Protestantism risks appearing so phobic about the possibility of seeming exclusive as to give an impression of standing for nothing beyond that which could win a nod of approval from most well-meaning, civic-minded people. It often seems that these churches are involved in a bidding war to see who can sign up the most adherents by soft-pedaling doctrinal affirmations and obligations connected to practicing the faith. Such churches give the impression that if one is at home in the culture, there is no reason one should not be entirely at home in the church. The question these churches are asking appears to be, who can offer the best deal to the would-be religious consumer?

Boundaries and the Virtue of Open-Mindedness

Boundaries come into play when it is necessary to stand for something, to have an identity specific enough that potential adherents know what they are getting into, and how and where that identity differs from alternatives and from the general culture. The notion of a clear identity is generally understood well enough when it comes to, say, Alcoholics Anonymous or the Heritage Foundation, but when it comes to a church unashamedly affirming specific doctrinal content, we Protestants are worried lest we be accused of not being open-minded. *Open-mindedness* ought to describe a generosity of spirit characterized by willingness to do the following: to learn from others, to try to welcome questions, to take the points of view of others seriously, to change one's mind when confronted with an unassailable argument, and, above all, to be aware of the fact that all human beings and every human institution is fallible. However, many Protestants today, in the name of open-mindedness, avoid openly affirming doctrines distinctive to the Christian gospel, lest they be judged insufficiently open-minded, a dreaded rebuke.

Those judged to be insufficiently open-minded may be pilloried as closed-minded or even *dogmatic*, a term derived from the same Greek *dokeo* from which comes one of the roots of the word *orthodox*. *Dogma* simply refers to approved teaching, although *dogmatic* has unfortunately become a term of reproach in secular and even in most Protestant use. Is it truly desirable that every mind be perpetually open? Is it acceptable that people and communities should never make up their minds about anything? Should no amount of study, reflection, or experience ever lead a person or community to risk a commitment? Since it is possible to be wrong about anything and everything, should a person or a community rule out ever reaching a point of conviction?

David Brooks has written about the skill required to navigate between the extremes of surrendering one's beliefs at the first whiff of opposition, on the one hand, and, on the other, holding on to a belief even when all the evidence is stacked against it. "The median point," he writes, "between flaccidity and rigidity is the virtue of firmness. The firm believer can build a steady worldview on solid timbers but still delight in new information."[8] Firmness—neither flaccidity nor rigidity—is a quality for which mainstream Protestants would do well to strive.

Granted, it is always risky to form a conviction, but all of life is about taking risks. The truly open mind is likely to be an empty mind—one that appears to avoid the risks of conviction by remaining perpetually uncommitted, which is to say, firmly committed to neutrality, or perhaps, indifference. Such persons are difficult to find, to say the least, and if such are found, they are unlikely to prove useful mentors. Even those most devoted to open-mindedness are clearly not averse to professing a conviction—in this case, about the necessity of being open-minded—which means, it would seem, committing to making up one's mind not to make up one's mind.

Faith in the triune God is not helpfully described in terms of either open-mindedness or closed-mindedness. The church understands itself as a community of people whom God has called together and united in Christ, rather than an ad hoc association of individuals temporarily joined on a spiritual or intellectual quest. (The Greek word *ecclesia* means "called out.") Faith begins with trust and is marked by affirmation, which may be embodied as doctrine, by guidelines for a church that teaches and mentors, as well as by communal practices.

It goes without saying that those who value orthodoxy are quite capable of being narrow, judgmental, and ungenerous, just as the fundamentalists, the liberals, the heterodox, the atheists, the progressives, the conservatives, the open-minded, the closed-minded, and anyone else may be, no matter what the label. It is also possible to embrace what some have called a "generous orthodoxy," which is not about enforcement as much as about affirmation. Orthodoxy need not glamorize the past or varnish over the sins of the church while it nevertheless receives with appreciation the gifts that have been handed on by our forebears in the greater church: affirmations rooted in the distinguishing landmarks of Word and Sacrament, Scripture, the ecumenical creeds, and responsible *episkopē*. It is with the help of these defining features of the church that we discover anew in every generation the things with which we have to do to serve our engagement with the living God: Father, Son, and Holy Spirit.

8. Brooks, "Mental Virtues."

To Which God Does Orthodoxy Point?

The point of orthodoxy is to point to this specific God in a culture in which there is already a lot of god-talk, much of it superficial and frivolous, and some of it downright scurrilous. The word *God* is so well known that we presume that everyone means the same thing by it. But clearly this is not the case. By God do we mean a sort of Santa Claus in the sky? Or do we refer to the tribal mascot whose greatness is proclaimed by suicide bombers? Or maybe we mean the Avenger on high who looks a lot like the Westboro Baptist Church, out to punish gay people? Or do we have in mind the caricature of the Judeo-Christian God despised by the "new atheists"? Or do we mean the friendly and abstract Deity to whom children are introduced in countless children's sermons? the sterile god of some philosophers; or the one who provides backup to any number of special-interest groups dedicated to repealing the twentieth and twenty-first centuries?

Those outside the church may, of course, honor any god or none at all, but for those who are united with the church, it is a different matter. Today's church is the heir of a faith that has been formed, shaped, and defined over many generations. We who are part of the church must maintain a significant measure of modesty in what we have to say about God, but the God of whom we dare to speak is the God revealed in the community, Israel and the church, whose experience of God is represented in Word and Sacrament, Scripture, the hard-won ecumenical creeds that exhibit earnest struggles to witness to God in human speech, and supported by church officers over the centuries who have done their best to keep the charge they have been given to guard the integrity of the faith the community has received. That is what orthodoxy is about: thoughtful, faithful zeal for the one, triune God.

The antonym of orthodoxy is not so much heterodoxy, although it is that, of course, but rather triviality. Some of the many historical and contemporary schisms and heresies might fairly be described as the pursuit of something trivial masquerading as so utterly essential as to justify splitting the church. More typically, trivialization is an ever-present threat within mainstream churches, including the mid-American generic variety. This is particularly true in an era when churches in general are on the defensive, frequently declining in numbers and influence, and frantically looking for ways to recover the strength and status so fondly remembered. Unfortunately, anxiety easily leads to the indiscriminate embracing of any and all fixes that promise to make it all better, and most of those fixes involve trivializing what is and ought to be anything but trivial. Trivializing looks different in so-called progressive settings than it does in so-called evangelical settings. But trivializing is trivializing. At the core of all trivializing is the domestication of the holy God.

At the heart of orthodox Christianity is the conviction that God's ways are not our ways, and God's thoughts are not our thoughts. Thus, to love, know, and serve God calls for humility. God's wisdom will always challenge conventional wisdoms of every sort. God's call to obedience will always put us in tension with other loyalties. To serve God will not always reward us with the applause of our neighbors. The God who, in Christ, is certainly and reliably *for* us sinners may also, in this or that instance, be against us—or at least against confusing God and God's agenda with ourselves and our own agendas. God is worthy of our profound respect and our attention. It is a matter for dismay when, in the church, God is reduced to a divine butler, or to the mascot invoked to support one side in the culture wars, or to a God interested only in the details of our personal salvation while indifferent to the rest of the created world and to injustice—to a God whose promise of a new creation, a new heaven and earth, has been whittled down to who goes to heaven and who doesn't.

The Triune God: Loving but Dangerous

In the U.S., people are friendly, and churches like to think of themselves as friendly. Is God friendly? Certainly the good news is that God loves us, and God may be an intimate companion, but the God of orthodox Christian faith ought not be so easily reduced to such a simple and benign status as friendly. God's love does not change the fact that love may take fierce forms. God is loving but dangerous too, and especially so when we need to be called to account. God's judgment is a necessary movement of divine love. Divine judgment takes us seriously and takes seriously principalities and powers, human or otherwise, that need to be opposed in order that they may be redeemed or overcome. The friendly, all-forgiving, domesticated God so familiar to American Protestantism is not the God of Bible or the church. One word, well known in Scripture, tradition, and liturgy, serves as an essential shorthand description of the triune God of the Bible and the church. That word is *holy*.

One who stumbles into a mid-American generic Protestant service would scarcely have any reason to perceive God as holy. The word may be sung because it is in the sung repertoire, or it may occasionally be used to address God. But *holy* does not go well with the deeply rooted American bias toward the casual and the democratic that extends even to deity. The columnist Leonard Pitts writes about a selfie posted on Twitter by a teenager mugging for the camera while visiting Auschwitz. He notes that neither is this is an unusual phenomenon, nor is it restricted to teenagers. It happens at the 9/11 memorial in New York City, at the Vietnam memorial in Washington DC, at the American cemetery in Normandy, and "at grandmother's funeral." Pitts comments that "this whole thing of mugging for cameras in inappropriate places feels viscerally . . . wrong. It suggests a cluelessness, a shallowness, and an incapacity for reverence that have come to feel like the signature of these times."[9] In the church, as well as in the larger culture, we seem to have lost the capacity for what one might call *gravitas*—a sense of deep respect.

When I was a pastor in Michigan, Metropolitan Filaret, chief officer of the Ukrainian Orthodox Church, visited our congregation when we were gathered for evening prayer. We met in the chapel. The center aisle led to a simple Communion Table that held a chalice and paten. A cross was mounted on the wall behind it. When Metropolitan Filaret entered the chapel, he bowed deeply before Table and cross, both representing the same Jesus Christ to whom our separate traditions bear witness. His gesture both moved me and made me want to join him in a human response that is profoundly appropriate when one senses and acknowledges the holy. To honor God as holy acknowledges a reverent distance between God and mortals that doesn't suit the contemporary temperament.

Mid-American generic Protestantism is about the horizontal rather than the vertical. Indeed, community—the horizontal—is terribly important, but not at the expense of the vertical. Christian faith is to be engaged with a big God, a holy God. The horizontal—turning our faces outward, toward the world to which God directs us—is difficult to sustain apart from the vertical: the sense that God is big enough, trustworthy enough to support us in the occasional victories and considerable disappointments we are bound to experience as we seek to reshape our corner of the world, at least, so that it may more nearly resemble the coming kingdom (reign) of God.

In our American Protestant world, it is perhaps prudent to place the accent on the horizontal—on doing good—because people in our culture are likely to respect it. Americans are usually ready to volunteer to tutor in a school, to get involved in a microlending program, to help build a Habitat

9. Pitts, "Talking Selfies."

house, or to join any number of organizations dedicated to influencing public policy. At such points, secular and Christian values overlap and reinforce each other. However, even though doing good needs no justification, nevertheless for Christians, doing good is an imperative that grows out of our faith, and our faith has doctrinal content. That content begins with the affirmation that the triune God has become incarnate—made flesh—in Jesus Christ, in whom we recognize that the material world is hallowed and that God has called us to take it and all its creatures, including our embodied fellow human beings, seriously. We have been called to be Christ's disciples, turning toward those to whom he turned: those in need of healing, of compassion, of companionship on the journey. When we make this turn, God joins our efforts to God's own mission to the world in Christ and, empowered by the Spirit, to point to God's promised new creation. At the same time, paradoxically, no social or political movement can safely be equated with God's kingdom.[10]

Doing Good and Being Good

But in doing good we run the risk of thinking of ourselves as good people, the ones who are the givers, somehow not like those who are the recipients of our benevolence. At this point it is urgent to revisit our theological basics. When we do good it is not because it is safe to think of ourselves as good. Like every human being, we are broken, susceptible to self-deception, on the defensive against needy neighbors, and not as familiar as we should be with repentance. Repentance is not a one-time affair but a lifelong living out of our baptism. We repent not as a kind of payoff to God, a gesture we owe as a prerequisite for forgiveness. Our baptism serves as God's solemn and gracious pledge that we are now a part of God's own servant people, living always in the assurance of forgiveness, strengthened by that assurance to take the kind of risks required for living boldly and courageously, because even in doing good, we will sometimes do harm. In our continuing repentance, we turn again and again with as much self-knowledge as we can bear, daring to trust that God is indeed big enough, strong enough to see us through, and, sometimes, to save others from our good intentions.

Insights drawn from the sixteenth-century Reformation and from subsequent Protestant experience have served us well enough, more or less, but not all invite continuing adherence. Protestantism began as a corrective

10. Ellul, *False Presence*.

movement within the church universal. Corrective movements are necessary, but over time it is not unusual for them to outlive the historical moment in which they were most relevant. What clearly serves as a correction in one time and context can be understood in other times and contexts as overcorrection. This is true, I think, of the so-called Protestant principle. Protestantism is wary both of idolatry and of false prophets, but the object of that wariness has all too often been equated with Roman Catholicism and everything that it calls to mind. The result has been that Protestantism in America, at least, has been unlikely to question its own habits of thinking, particularly when it comes to romanticizing individual authority and overreacting in suspicion of communal authority. We are out of balance. It is no wonder that, to those conditioned to generic Protestantism, orthodoxy smells like something alien, characterized by uniformity and coercion rather than rich complexity and affirmation.

PART 2

3

Mid-American Generic Protestant Worship

IT IS REASONABLE, I think, to presume that what we believe matters when we pray, and also that how we pray is important in identifying what we believe. If we cannot pray our theology, it needs to be questioned. Orthodoxy, understood as "rich complexity and affirmation," rests upon a foundation that is liturgical as well as theological, calling for worship that is "rooted deeply enough in the church's ecosystem to give life to the wonderfully rich affirmations of the gospel."[1] How are we doing with that?

The Protestant principle has a role to play, as does self-criticism generally, but it can be overdone. No human artifact—our artifacts include our theologies and our liturgies—is infallible or untouchable, but some have deeper roots and a more compelling case to make than others. The Protestant reflex is to presume that the prophetic privilege of questioning anything that enjoys widespread consensus implies a duty to find the weakness or error that must surely underlie the consensus, and expose it. In the case of liturgy shaped by classical historical and theological norms, the American version of generic Protestantism is inclined to be suspicious, doubting that these have any authoritative claim on our attention or consideration, choosing instead to privilege local or pastoral laissez-faire. For those who see no relation between the basic affirmations of the church and the ways it

---

1. See p. 1 above.

worships on the Lord's Day, it really does not matter much what the church does when it gathers on Sunday morning.

A Calendar Conflict

A large mainline church in our neighborhood has run into a calendar conflict. Mother's Day and Pentecost occur on the same day! It provokes a dilemma: how to deal with this? The decision was made to observe Mother's Day on the same day as the general public, and to defer Pentecost for a week or two. Does God care? Probably not. But the decision tells us something about the congregation, or at least the leadership of the congregation. What it tells us is that pastor and church board are more likely to get in trouble with the most people if they soft-pedal Mother's Day, which is, of course, not a day honored in the liturgical calendar, but in the civil calendar—a Hallmark holiday, if you will. On the other hand, few know or care much about Pentecost—though it is certainly a key holiday in the liturgical year—and therefore, deferring it (or skipping it entirely) will not likely lead to intimidating restlessness in the pews.

So, if God probably doesn't care, why should we? Maybe we should care because it offers such a vivid illustration of how the general culture is likely to prevail whenever it comes into conflict with a church culture meant to be formed in response to the gospel and attuned to its rhythms. Or maybe we should care because this example illustrates so well the depth of the challenge to mainline churches to rethink our role as mentors to our own people—our role both to hand on the rudiments of the Christian story effectively and to encourage the faithful to engage their imaginations as they live into the story. Or maybe we should care about our example of calendar conflict because it illustrates so well how easy it is for churches to be seduced by the sentimental—as though sentiment and faith are the same thing, or at least mutually reinforcing.

It is possible to acknowledge Mother's Day without diverting the whole liturgy into a paean to motherhood. Prayer can be offered for mothers, and for those who have lost their mothers, and for those whose mothering skills prove useful outside domestic settings even when they have no children of their own. But not all the prayers need to focus on motherhood, nor do the hymns, the Scripture readings, or the sermon. To place the focus on Pentecost—the last of the great fifty days of Easter, the day that recalls the birth of the church, when the gifts of the Spirit flooded upon the apostles and overflowed their testimony—makes a statement about what story takes priority in the church.

I am immensely grateful for the Revised Common Lectionary. A sermon should certainly start with a specific text, rather than a completely autonomous idea legitimized by a verse here and there. Nevertheless, it might be possible even on Pentecost to hear a sermon on motherhood linked to the Acts 2:1–21 text, as hard to imagine as that may be; but more often than not, such a sermon will be a cause for dismay. Unfortunately, it is not unusual for a lectionary text to serve the preacher as the source of an idea, or whole set of ideas, which provides a springboard for a sermon that leaves the text behind. The text, having served its ostensible purpose, neither shapes nor controls the sermon, for once it has sparked an idea, the text is no longer necessary. And, sadly, it is frequently the case that the Lord of the text is left behind in the same obscurity to which the text has been relegated.

Preaching Is a Sacramental Act

Those who would preach often find that the churches they serve have been conditioned to hold certain expectations for the sermon. The congregation may expect the sermon to be either a lecture on some religious topic, or exhortations to do certain things. In some cases sermons are expected to be a form of therapy, editorial commentary on public issues, or entertaining or tear-jerking stories. A sermon that is deeply rooted in a text and that vividly evokes the Lord of the text may do any or all those things, but they are all side effects, not the main purpose of preaching. The sermon is meant to be sacramental: to use words and verbal images as a vehicle by which the Holy Spirit may make manifest the presence of the risen Christ in the assembly. One reason that it so often fails to do so is that the preacher has set out to do something else. And, if the preacher has set out to do something else, it is often because the preacher's experience in the church from childhood on has been that sermons have been employed to do something else. It is particularly hard to imagine preaching as a sacramental act when sacraments have been minimized or banished to the margins of our worship. The diminishment of sacramental life has had the unintended consequence of distorting and thus diminishing preaching. When preaching is not sacramental, and the sacraments themselves are minimized or didacticized, then worship evolves into giving information, motivational speech, group therapy or a (restrained) pep rally—none of which have anything much to do with a meeting with the holy God.

Ritual . . . Bad!

In much of mid-American generic Protestantism, worship has been perceived to be an arena for religious instruction, or for exerting emotional pressure in hopes of persuading the distant or the reluctant to make a spiritual commitment of one sort or another. Worship has been seen as a forum where a group of individuals gather to do personal devotional exercises in public. These are the sorts of things that are left when we have inherited a tradition that tells us that ritual is ritualism, and that ritualism is bad. We have heard that ritual is bad, perhaps even idolatrous, because it elevates doing prescribed things above thinking about things or stirring up pious feelings. Ritual is bad because it is possible to go through the motions on automatic pilot. Ritual is bad because it can leave you self-satisfied at having shown up for a "religious" event that has nothing to do with what is in your heart or mind, but that presumably polishes your public image.

However, ritualism is in the eye of the beholder. *Ritualism* is a pejorative term used to disparage someone else's ritual. It is normally employed by those who mistakenly imagine that it is possible to be both Christian and ritual-free. To make an accusation of ritualism is basically to make a charge of hypocrisy, of hiding indifference or lack of faith behind a pretense of piety. Certainly it is possible for those who claim to be devout to be hypocrites, or at least to be participating in worship for reasons other than the stated purpose of the liturgy, and that holds true whether the rite is either elaborate or utterly simple. However, an accusation of hypocrisy is probably one best left to the only judge who is infallible, especially when it is a judgment leveled against a whole community. It is legitimate to critique ritual, but a critique needs to be based on informed judgment, something other than simple distaste for or suspicion of the unfamiliar.

A Requiem Mass was offered for President John F. Kennedy at St. Matthew's Cathedral in Washington on November 25, 1963. The liturgy was in Latin in those days, shortly before the Second Vatican Council's reforms instituted the use of the vernacular in Roman Catholic worship. A Protestant observer watched on television as Kennedy's widow, Jacqueline Kennedy, took her place in the pew. The observer could not imagine how this service, in a foreign language, could possibly offer any support or comfort to Mrs.

Kennedy or any other worshiper. But all at once, the penny dropped, and the observer experienced a new insight. The observer realized that this was not the first time the widow had heard these Latin words, or the first time she had observed the rites of which the mass is composed. As a woman with a Catholic education, Mrs. Kennedy probably was familiar enough with the text of the liturgy that she had at least a good idea of what the Latin words meant, but even if she had no idea at all, the cadences, the tones, and the ritual acts combined to convey a profoundly familiar act of worship that had been deeply etched into her soul over a lifetime. In her grief and pain, it is unlikely that she would have been able to draw more comfort if the service had been in English, because it was not an occasion that was likely to be enhanced by the processing of language. She was present as a worshiper in a communal act addressed to God, not as a consumer of religious information or public consolation directed toward her. The ritual spoke to the heart first, the mind second, if it needed to speak to the mind at all.

On that sad morning, our Protestant observer intuited what has been made more apparent in the relatively new discipline of ritual studies. Worship is about more than processing words. Rites mean something, and the meaning can be pondered, reflected upon, and even explained to a point, but the meaning is embodied in the action, in the doing of the rite. Trying to explain it while it is going on certainly kills the rite. The time for talking about it is either afterward or beforehand. Worship is holistic, involving the whole self, not always or only the conscious mind. It speaks in a language that includes movement, action, silence, taste, and sight, sometimes accompanied by words.

To some extent, at least some Protestants owe their prejudice against anything that might be described as ritual to the Puritan heritage, but it also derives from the all-embracing Enlightenment era that has furnished the "reigning plausibility structure" for our culture for more than the past four centuries. Everything from revival meetings to the contemporary version of them that sees worship as an instrument of a utilitarian purpose such as either explaining things or arousing emotion contributes to the idea that rite must give way to a calculated, pragmatic approach. The marginalization of the sacraments, only beginning to be reversed in the twentieth and twenty-first centuries by Episcopalians and Lutherans in particular, with Presbyterians and United Methodists far behind but catching up in some places, has played a huge role in legitimizing the sort of flat rationalism that disdains rite in favor of worship imagined to be ritual-free.

Ritual . . . Bad?

A lay advisor working with youth in a large Protestant congregation had grown up Roman Catholic. One of her tasks involved assisting various teams of high school students responsible for planning and leading worship at the beginning of every Sunday evening meeting. She commented to a member of the ministry staff that as a former Catholic, she was continually amazed that the highest priority of the youth planning worship was novelty: never the same words twice; never do anything the way you did it last time. Why this need for something new? Chalk it up to the classic suspicion of ritual so deeply embedded in generic Protestantism. To mean something, the words must be, if not entirely spontaneous, at least not composed very long beforehand, or certainly not found in an official book. Novelty serves as the essential sign of authenticity.

However, if you have not visited a patient in a nursing home when a visiting pastor has come to lead a service of worship, you have perhaps missed something important. A patient who has had years of experience as a regular worshiper may not know where she is, or even recognize her own children or grandchildren, yet when a familiar hymn is begun, the patient is likely to join in, knowing both text and tune by heart. Could the patient explain the meaning of the hymn text? No. The hymn has been deeply absorbed, woven into the texture of the patient's unconscious—one might say, into the soul—permitting, but not requiring, a connection with the conscious mind. When the patient first encountered the hymn, perhaps she pondered the meaning of the words, and in singing the hymn now and then over the years, it is likely that she may have consciously reflected on the meaning of the text at least occasionally. But the significance of the hymn does not lie in one's ability to focus with laser-like precision on the meaning of the words, as though the hymn were primarily about communicating information. The meaning is in the entire phenomenon of the hymn—not only the words, but also the music and the physical act of singing it communally in particular settings. The hymn does not mean less when sung by an Alzheimer's patient.

Another patient, even one whose cognition is cloudy, will join in readily when the worship leader begins the Apostles' Creed: "I believe in God, the Father Almighty . . ."; or the Nicene: "We believe in one God . . ." Those pastors accustomed to presiding at funerals or memorial services for members of a certain generation may have discovered that many of those present for the service are able to join in the King James Version of Psalm

23 without missing a word. Are they to be faulted if they are not thinking, thinking, thinking about its meaning word for word as they say it? The meaning lies in the act of reciting it together, quite apart from whatever level of intellectual scrutiny is applied at the moment.

Not only those living with mental impairments, but worshipers of any age who live with cognitive disabilities may be able to join in those parts of the liturgy that nearly everybody knows from memory: When the presider says, "The Lord be with you," they will answer, "And also with you." To know these responses that occur throughout a liturgical service is to know the structure, the architecture, of the liturgy, which is also the basic structure of the Christian faith. Certainly one "knows" not only with an active intellect, however much additional pleasure it gives to be able to use that cognitive resource. One "knows" at many levels—unconscious as well as conscious—without relying exclusively on a single fragile gift. When the liturgy is always created de novo for the place and occasion, repetition is devalued in favor of what appears to be spontaneity.

Is Spontaneity Spontaneous?

The gift of crafting the language of worship in such a way that a congregation can own it has not been distributed in equal measure to all who attempt it. While it is possible to add the amen to a prayer uttered by one person even if the language is awkward, it becomes much more difficult for members of a congregation to add their own voices to the liturgical use of printed texts composed by someone who has neither a gift for it nor an understanding of the poetic nature of such texts. The following text of a responsive Call to Worship for Easter Sunday was obviously written in-house, even though the congregation that used it is part of a denomination that has an official book of worship and other liturgical resources. These liturgical resources offer examples far more biblically, theologically, and liturgically sensitive than this Call to Worship, not to mention more attuned to the needs of people expected to speak in unison.

> Easter begins in despair! Our life, our love, our hope seem dead in the tomb.
> **Who will roll away the stone?**
> Easter takes us by surprise. How great is the day when evil and death are defeated!
> **To the fallen, help is offered! To those who mourn, great joy is given!**

> To the broken and despairing, hope is offered!
> **To those in darkness, light appears! To the whole world, life and peace are offered!**
> Christ is risen!
> **Christ is risen, indeed! Alleluia!**

These words psychologize rather than theologize. The text presumes to be able to say how members of the congregation feel. They are required to ask a meaningless rhetorical question. The lines are framed in long lines of prose that are difficult for a congregation to say together. Much of the text is in the passive voice, and so the text gives no clear indication of who offers help; gives joy to the mourning; brings light, hope, life, and peace. Finally this Call to Worship uses too many exclamation points! True, this Call to Worship meets the expectations of those who want novelty, of those who feel that to use a form of words anyone on earth has ever used before betrays a lack of authenticity. True, no one in the congregation will read these words as though the words had been read a thousand times before, and it is not likely that this Call to Worship will ever be used again anywhere. Would it have been too difficult to find words from Scripture to serve the purpose of anchoring the liturgy in language of the deep tradition? The last two lines work well enough all by themselves:

> Christ is risen!
> Christ is risen indeed! Alleluia!

Even the intellectually impaired can learn, absorb, repeat, and engage with such a simple call and response. When those who plan worship privilege novelty, the long-term result will be that no one will ever be able to participate actively in worship unless they are gifted with clear minds and the ability to decipher the printed page, and little of what is said in worship will be impressed upon the deep memory.

The labored Call to Worship above is an example of a ritual whose didactic tone seems intended to support the masquerade that it is ritual-free. The Call to Worship appears ritual-free because it did not come from a book; it appears ritual-free because it was produced for one-time use in a specific congregation for a particular occasion; and it appears ritual-free because no one could possibly say the words on automatic pilot while gazing around, while not paying attention, or while in a fog of mental confusion. But to describe the language of this Call to Worship as ritual-free requires us to consent to a very narrow definition of ritual. It is not, in fact, ritual-free.

Everything done in an assembly for worship fits under the rubric of ritual, even when none of it is written down and none of it is officially required. In an assembly of people, even silence has to be organized and coordinated. Spontaneity is rarely truly spontaneous, and novelty is rarely novel. Any service in any church tends to follow certain familiar protocols, even if they are not written down.

Every particular community assembled for worship has learned from experience to expect certain things to happen, usually in a predictable sequence, and even when variations might be introduced for the sake of novelty, these elements will be drawn from a known repertoire. Ways of framing prayers, and spoken responses or exclamations that seem to be spontaneous have been learned over time by observation and repetition. Postures, movements, tones of voice and cadences of speech are as likely to be predictable in a Pentecostal service as at a High Mass, a Quaker meeting, or the new service added specifically to appeal to millennials. No service is ritual-free. The question is not whether a gathering for worship is a ritual or not. The questions are rather these: Whose ritual is this? What presumptions does it make about those who will use it? How does it characterize God? How does it use language, movement, repetition, and gesture to communicate its meaning to young and old, to those of sound mind and to those whose mental processes are immature or impaired? And what *does* it mean?

Who or What Will Offer Protection from Idiosyncratic Liturgy?

Even in Roman Catholic, Episcopal, and Lutheran services that are highly scripted, the presiding minister's role makes a huge difference in the way the liturgy is enacted. A service from the Book of Common Prayer can be led carelessly, with little advance planning, in a way that may mute the elegance of the language or draw too much attention to the personality of the presider. And yet, even so, the texts of the liturgy are in place, representing the deep tradition of the church. The presider's performance of the liturgy may be distracting or sloppy, but the faith of the church cannot be entirely obscured even so, because it is nevertheless represented in the texts and rubrics. In many Protestant churches, even in some whose denominations have thoughtfully crafted official liturgies, the only texts and rubrics actually in use are either those passed down by observation or texts and rubrics created exclusively by the current pastor. Congregations learn over time to grow accustomed to the fact that a change of pastorate brings with it a change in liturgy—sometimes for the better, sometimes not. When the pastor exercises so much influence, and when following a specific liturgy is not required either by rule or by tradition, no intermediary protects the congregation from an idiosyncratic liturgy that may represent the pastor's faith but may poorly represent the church's faith.

One of the key issues of the Reformation was the conviction of the reformers that the liturgy ought to be in the vernacular rather than in Latin. For the Reformed (Genevan-based) reformers in particular, it was considered important that worshipers understand the liturgy—not just the spoken language but the meaning that lay behind it. They made efforts to catechize the faithful to that purpose. However, neither Lutherans nor Reformed nor Anglicans left the language or practice of public worship to the insights or skills of individual pastors alone. Rather, leaders prepared fixed liturgies meant to be authoritative, to be used exactly as composed, with minimal opportunity for extemporaneous contributions. Why? Because the reformers recognized that any and every liturgy embodied some representation of the Christian gospel, whether thoughtfully, deliberately, and intentionally; or carelessly and unintentionally. That was true then, and it is true now.

Some pastors, in this era accustomed to so-called seeker services created by and for the baby-boomer generation, believe that the essence of Protestant worship is that it be understandable. The new pastor may not institute a new service for seekers but nevertheless may be committed to explaining everything and reducing the vocabulary of worship to language that has been flattened out, gutted of metaphor and nuance—language close to the same kind used to give directions to a stranger in the neighborhood who is looking for the grocery store.

However, at no time in the early history of the church was its Lord's Day liturgy intentionally designed for persons not a part of the worshiping community. Evangelistic services (twentieth- or twenty-first-century "seeker services") may be worship of a sort, but they are created for a specific target audience of people who may be led to faith but who are not presumed to share it yet. When the new pastor decides that the purpose of the church's liturgy is to be ritual-free and is to include explanatory language so that a first-time visitor might be persuaded to be a Christian, the congregation is forced to worship as though they too are among the uncommitted observers, the uncertain novices trying to wrap their heads around the mystery of

Christian faith as though they had never been exposed to it before. What is intended as simplicity is actually simplistic, misleading newcomers and depriving the faithful of the full range of spiritual nourishment embodied in a richer liturgy of Word and Sacrament.

In North American society, we believe that all people are created equal—that is to say, equal before God and equal before the law. To believe in equality does not mean to believe that everyone is equally prepared to take a class in calculus without finishing any prerequisites, or to understand the faith of the church upon first being exposed to its worship. When a pastor or educator takes a youth group to visit a mosque, synagogue, or Buddhist temple, it will be expected that someone will interpret what it is that worshipers are doing there. It is not elitist to presume that, for most things worth understanding, instant comprehension is unlikely, and preparation is necessary. Christian faith is utterly simple in some respects, having to do with the love of God and deep respect for the neighbor. But the world is complex, and life is complicated, and love itself is not always simple, nor can it be summoned on command. The gospel involves the telling of stories, and hearing the stories requires becoming acquainted with the contexts in which the stories are told, and the stories themselves may refer to things that cannot so much be understood as grasped intuitively. Language, with its use of similes, metaphors, and paradox, juxtaposing poetic uses with straightforward prose, evokes the use of the imagination in a way that enables an intuitive sense of a meaning that is layered, rich, and complex.

The language of the liturgy is sometimes biblical language and sometimes other language in the same key. The Christian faith as exhibited in the Bible or as embodied in classic liturgical language is deep enough and broad enough to be worthy of lifelong reflection. It is not a neutral language but a language of love, one that overflows whatever words it may use, and it is no surprise that those exposed to it for the first time may not get it, even though some may be curious enough or intrigued enough to want to explore it further. The language of worship and the gospel embodied in it matters for the baptized, and serves neither them nor the serious seeker when it is supplanted by a prosaic substitute—language reduced to nothing more than a tool to provide information, as though the gospel might be made instantly accessible. Worship may possess drawing power for some who are exposed to it, but evangelism is not the purpose of the church's liturgy.

Body Language

By using the word *language* in the heading above, I may seem to be endorsing a liturgy mainly centered on the processing of words. But that is not my intention. In addition to spoken language there is the language of rite (body language, if you will): that which is done rather than just said. The Lord's Day liturgy is like dance. We bring our bodies to it as well as our minds, including muscle memory. Beneath it is a kind of heartbeat, a rhythm, keeping time. Everyone has a role in the dance, and the roles are coordinated, even though not always in unison. The role of each is essential to the whole. Dance is work, but it is also liberating, and permits us to explore postures and positions we would not attempt by ourselves. It subtly tells a story into which we may insert ourselves, experimentally. At the same time, it both expresses and evokes emotions, whether our own or some we would like to try on. One enters into the dance as a discipline, because this is what we have committed to do, and it is time to do it, whether our inner mood matches the outward expression of the dance or not. While we are engaged in it, the clock is not important. The dance means something, but the meaning is intuited in the doing of it, and explanations of its meaning are something entirely different, and not a substitute for actually engaging in the dance.

Rooted in Jewish experience and the ministry of Jesus, Christian worship from as early as we know anything about it has been a composition of a Word proclaimed in and for the assembly and a meal shared. Word and Sacrament embrace a whole choreography of actions: singing, speaking, hearing, seeing, opening the book, silence, breaking, pouring, anointing, lifting a hand, laying on of hands, bowing, processing, kneeling, eating and drinking, blessing accompanied by gestures as well as words. Those Protestants whose worship has been formed by the habit of excluding the body, or of reducing its participation to a minimum: sitting, standing, listening, speaking and singing, may imagine that the reforms that instituted this restrained bodily engagement are purer than a fulsome practice that has been written off as more sensuous than spiritual. But they are wrong. Some Protestant worship runs the risk of drawing an unwarranted dividing line between that which is material and that which is spiritual, as though our faith were not rooted in the incarnation. To be spiritual presumably requires minimizing art, color, bodily movement, and even eating and drinking—as though what God desires is for us to worship in our minds, not distracted by our bodies. Protestants need to let go that dualistic mythology, because it is not only a false definition of *spiritual*, but it is profoundly unbiblical.

One reason that this body/spirit dualism has flourished in some forms of Protestantism is that we have inherited the idea that all you need for authentic worship is a worshipful disposition, a heartfelt faith. The argument is that we don't need anything else, because true worship is related to spiritual feelings, not ritual. Once you accept these premises, it doesn't matter much what is done or not done in worship. It is not hard to imagine where this mythology comes from. It is rooted in a distorted view of the reformers' work to simplify the medieval Mass, which had become intricate and inaccessible. Simplification was also advanced by the Puritans, who found the worship of the seventeenth- and eighteenth-century Church of England cold and sterile, as well they might have. Clergy often read the liturgy as though the most important thing was to get through all the words, and the people's role was simply to listen patiently. The sermons were prepared not by the local pastor but by an offsite cleric and were distributed to parishes to be read aloud, and it was not unusual for the same sermons to be recycled. The typical service was Morning Prayer. Eucharist was celebrated only occasionally. The Puritan critique served as an attempt at correction, calling for a worship designed to invite involvement, warm engagement. The Puritan critique and its effects on Protestant worship since provide a good example of how correctives that make perfect sense at the time do not necessarily serve us well in another context.

An Overcorrection That Needs to Be Revisited

I do not believe that worship is valid only if the proper feelings are present. If proper spiritual feelings were prerequisite, then at least half the pastors either would not be able to be present on a given Sunday or would have to be present under false pretenses. The choir would be missing voices, the ushers would be understaffed, while parents undone by a recalcitrant child or two would have to turn around and go back home.

No doubt it is true that a worshipful disposition can overcome obstacles, including poor preaching, indifferent music, unattractive worship spaces, a detached congregation, and poorly planned or badly enacted liturgy. But it is also true that a worshipful disposition can be discouraged and even extinguished by a liturgical environment that provides no support for it, while it is equally true that the proper support can evoke a worshipful disposition and can encourage and strengthen it. The church's liturgy both expresses faith and forms it. Some will be present whose inward disposition indeed finds its expression in the liturgy. Yet in every assembly there will also be present those for whom the liturgy serves to kindle faith that may be feeble or absent, and begins to give shape to it. Many of us wear one disposition this Sunday, and put on another disposition the next.

Faith is seldom a steady state. It expands and flourishes, then retreats, by turns. Authentic worship does not require that everyone assembled bring to it a robust faith all at the same time. People of deep commitment may find themselves at a low point in their life of faith, not sure whether any of it is true or any of it matters, but they keep the discipline of the Lord's Day nevertheless, in the hope that God may touch them, if only for a moment, as they take their place in the worshiping assembly—if not this Sunday, then the next, or the next. Those church officers who are responsible for planning and executing worship are entrusted with providing a liturgical environment that embodies in words and action the faith of the church. Faith may survive intact if they fail in that responsibility, because God is not utterly dependent on our knowledge or skills, but it is not prudent to put God to the test.

Providing a liturgy that both expresses and impresses the faith of the church is a challenge when it is imagined that such a liturgy has to be created from scratch every Sunday, when it is thought that we must try hard not to repeat ourselves—as though novelty might pass as spontaneity, and as though an appearance of spontaneity might pass as the pure gift of the Spirit. However, there is no need to start over again every week. Familiarity can be a vehicle for the Spirit. Some degree of repetition, far from being an offense, helps to write the gospel on the mind and spirit, and assists worshipers to intuit the heart of Christian faith, to internalize it and make it their own. James K. A. Smith contends that "quite simply, there is no formation without repetition," and he notes that "secular liturgies"—(think commercialism in all its forms, for example the stadium, the mall, and the arena, as well as popular culture in its many incarnations)—are shamelessly repetitive and spectacularly effective.[2]

---

2. Smith, *Imagining*, 183.

Liturgical Inculturation

The mainstream Protestant denominations are likely to have official liturgical books or guidelines and resources that are typically drawn from the ecumenical church, reflecting liturgical traditions deeply rooted in history, the experience of the larger church, thoughtful theological reflection, and the Bible. How do worship planners make use of such resources? Should they use them exactly as printed, following the rubrics as carefully as possible? Or should they use, for example, *The United Methodist Book of Worship* as a source from which to pull out a prayer or a litany when one is needed in a hurry? I do not find fault with those who choose to use the denomination's official liturgy exactly as printed, particularly knowing that most of the orders provide options at various points. But I also appreciate the fact that liturgies need to be adapted to local cultures. Adaptation includes thoughtful attention to enacting worship in ways that help to liberate liturgies from a preserved state on the printed page. At the same time, a denomination's book of worship is more than just a collection of liturgical pieces that can be lifted out of context to be used here and there, now and then. An ecology of the whole needs to be respected. James K. A. Smith observes, "Here we need to raise a critical, and perhaps uncomfortable, point: *form matters*—not because of any traditionalism or conservative preservation of the status quo, but precisely because . . . there is a logic to a practice that is unarticulated but nonetheless has a coherent 'sense' about it. Form matters because it is the form of worship that tells the Story (or better, *enacts* the Story)."[3]

Those officers who are specifically charged with planning worship for a congregation need to understand the ecology of the whole liturgy. When a planner gets the picture of the whole movement of the liturgy—central rites of Word and Eucharist, preceded by rites of gathering and followed by rites of sending—it is possible to re-create this whole with fidelity for a particular congregation without necessarily replicating it word for word or gesture for gesture. Words, music, and actions can be faithful to the official liturgy and at the same time respectful of the character of the local culture. The worship of a downtown church and of one in the suburbs or the country may draw from the same liturgical sources and each re-create them with integrity even though they may look, feel, and sound different because they are being enacted in very different cultural settings. One uses video projection while one relies only on print. One uses an instrumental combo or a

---

3. Ibid., 168.

piano while another uses an organ. In one congregation, members bow and make the sign of the cross, while in another they raise their hands in the air and offer spontaneous acclamations. One presumes formality, another informality. Respecting the deep liturgical tradition of the ecumenical church serves to embody the church's historic faith for each, but does not require uniformity in the execution of it.

While it is certainly possible for those who know the shape and basic theological moves of the classical liturgy to inculturate it both faithfully and appropriately, local autonomy when it comes to liturgical practice places huge burdens on the pastor, too often without sufficient preparation or mentoring. To inculturate the classical liturgy successfully requires something that has proven difficult, especially when positive role models of it are scarce—and that is to provide adequate preparation and support for those officers whose work it is to plan and lead worship in the local congregation.

Obstacles to a Faithful Inculturation of the Liturgy

In my own denomination, the Presbyterian Church (U.S.A.), a Directory for Worship is part of the constitution of the church. The Directory provides in compressed form a sophisticated historical and theological understanding of the classic liturgy of Word and Sacrament, and describes that liturgy in form and content. Candidates for ordination must pass an exam in Worship and Sacraments, based largely on the Directory. In addition, we have a Book of Common Worship (BCW) that provides excellent examples of complete liturgies. The problem is that once the candidate has passed the ordination exam, there are few positive imperatives that motivate the newly ordained and installed pastor to pay any further attention to the Directory or the BCW. Further, denominational authorities do not choose to make liturgical *episkopē* a priority. It is far more likely that a pastor will shape the liturgy for a congregation either by following whatever precedents have already been established in that place, or by following the example of a childhood pastor or campus minister. If the pastor believes that change is required, he or she will turn to the latest book or article that advocates forms of worship intended as evangelism or recruitment of new members. Or a pastor may use all these methods. Rarely are any of those models informed by attention to the history and theology embodied in the classical liturgy or, for that matter, for the pastor to have been trained well enough to be able to distinguish what might be optional from what is surely imperative.

While the pastor's authority over the liturgy is theoretically limited and shared with ordained elders, the truth is that these other church officers are not likely to know more about it than the pastor, and the pastor's influence will prevail more often than not. Under these circumstances, which are not too different from those in some other Protestant denominations, we are likely to suffer from too much local improvisation, with too prominent a role for the pastor, who has been handicapped by insufficient guidance and mentoring by the larger church.

Traditioning Faithfully

It is particularly at this point that mainstream Protestants do well to break with mid-American generic Protestant traditions, and profit by learning from Roman Catholics and the Orthodox as well as from Reformation models. In these churches, the liturgy is valued as resting at the very center of the church's life and animating it. Here is where the devotion of the faithful is formed and the deepest affirmations of the church embodied in such a way as to play a major role in handing on (traditioning) the substance of faith and pointing a direction for the ministries meant to flow from it. Such content is not so much explained as absorbed. Systematic reflection about it comes at another time; and, when it is absorbed, it begins to shape what one loves and how one lives in and for the world.

Most of those Protestants whose roots are closest to the Reformation value the central affirmations of the faith, represented in the ecumenical creeds and in a long history of ecumenical reflection on the story they tell and the affirmations they make. Yet for all practical purposes none of that seems to matter much when it comes to the liturgy. Even in churches officially distant from mid-American generic Protestantism, doctrine matters in putting together curriculum requirements for ministry preparation; it matters for the ecclesiastical bodies charged with scrutinizing the faith and preparation of candidates for ordination; it matters for preaching; but the prevailing presumption seems to be that doctrine doesn't matter all that much when it comes to the liturgy—what we do when we assemble for worship on the Lord's Day. But James K. A. Smith is rightly skeptical of the notion that "the historical, received forms of Christian worship" are "a kind of disposable husk than can be shucked (and chucked!) as long as we keep the kernel of the gospel 'message.'"[4]

4. Ibid.

The sense that "form" and "message" (liturgy and doctrine) are not intimately related is unintentionally reinforced when those who exercise *episkopē* in a denomination are likely not to exercise much oversight when it comes to the liturgical practice of congregations under their care. And yet, the Roman Catholics and the Orthodox are right to understand that the liturgy is where the congregation most profoundly meets and engages with the gospel and the Lord of the gospel. Perfection is unnecessary, and no liturgy approaches perfection. The congregation may meet the risen Christ in spite of liturgical imperfections—even in or in spite of its serious gaps. But, the form and content of the liturgy matter, and its form and contents will, for better or worse, shape a community's faith, its identity, and its way of being in the world. Even good preaching cannot counter the effects of a liturgy created from scratch, indifferent to what is missing. A liturgy that takes seriously the form and content of the classical liturgies commends to those regularly exposed to it the faith that the church has received, nourished, and handed on, and helps to sustain it.

The historic liturgies, Eastern and Western, are formed in such a way as to honor the vertical as well as the horizontal dimensions of the faith. In other words, they are capable of projecting the sense that we are dealing with a holy God. If our worship is not first and foremost centered on God, and specifically on the triune God, then it either falls short of worship or, worse, misdirects it. Mainstream Protestants need to reconsider views of worship that have been influenced by knee-jerk suspicion of Roman Catholics and Orthodox, or by the experimental revivalist movement of the nineteenth century and its contemporary offspring, or by psychological rather than theological approaches to worship. We also need to be wary of the entrepreneurial methods derived from the church-growth movement. An orthodox faith has need of an orthodox liturgy.

4

What's at Stake on Sunday Morning?

Christ Our Liturgist

AN ORTHODOX FAITH HAS need of an orthodox liturgy. What is *liturgy*, anyway? The word itself is unfamiliar in many Protestant congregations, and often signals something mysterious and alien. *Liturgy* is a compound of two Greek words: *leitos* ("public") and *ergon* ("work"), thus "public work." Maxwell Johnson says, "It is a secular Greek term for a *public* work done not by but on *behalf* of the people by another person or group appointed to that task."[1] The word does not mean "the work of the people," as so often said. "In fact," Johnson declares, "in the New Testament the primary use of this term is for Christ himself, whom the Letter to the Hebrews (8:2) designates precisely as our *leitourgos*."[2] In other words, Christ is our liturgist. Liturgy, then, "in the words of Nathan Mitchell, is '*opus Dei*,' something 'beautiful that God does for us.'"[3] Clearly, while the gathered assembly does things in worship, the primary actor in worship is the triune God.

Those who have the time and persistence to visit a variety of Protestant churches will discover vast differences in what happens in their assemblies, usually on Sunday morning. Here one may clearly see the effects

---

1. Johnson, *Praying and Believing*, xi.
2. Ibid., xii.
3. Mitchell, "The Amen Corner," 557–58, as cited in Johnson, xiii.

of the Protestant principle at work. Even more variations will be noted if the visitor were to observe formal or informal services during the week, or at church camps or retreats, or gatherings for worship on school or university campuses. They are likely to have in common some form of prayer, acts of praise, thanksgiving, and petition; and reading from the Bible. A service may be simple or elaborate, aesthetically complex or spare, emotionally extravagant or subtle, engaging multiple senses or just a few, overtly Christian or less obviously so. Many variations notwithstanding, these are all clearly examples of Christian communities at worship, but not everything that happens on Sunday morning should be described as the liturgy of the church.

Using that description in its most literal sense, there is in fact no one liturgy of the church but only multiple liturgies. Nevertheless, the historic Lord's Day liturgies, from those that are ancient to those of the Reformation and beyond, have certain features in common, and it is not Gregorian chant or Bach or candles or reading things from the printed page. All four Gospels follow a sequence that begins with baptism, then proclamation in word and action, followed by a climactic meal. In accord with this sequence, Gordon Lathrop has identified the central features of the Lord's Day liturgy in the simplest language possible: "bath, table, and word," along with attentiveness to the poor.[4] In ecclesiastical language these refer, of course, to baptism, Scripture and preaching, and the Holy Eucharist, all undertaken with the poor in mind, which includes gathering resources for those in need. The simplicity of the language helps us to focus on the key things but is not meant to leave out the fact that worship centered on Scripture, preaching, and sacraments (while attentive to the poor) will be embodied in specific forms that include prayerful praise, thanksgiving, and intercessions, and some of it will be sung. This very basic *ordo* is rooted in Scripture, particularly in the ministry of Jesus, but with Old Testament roots as well, and has been affirmed by Orthodox, Roman Catholics, and those Protestants historically linked to the magisterial Reformation. I think it is fair to identify these key things as, in substance, what it means to speak of the "liturgy of the church."

---

4. Lathrop, *Holy Things*, 89 (and elsewhere).

What Is a "Liturgy of the Church"?

It is true that none of these historic traditions can claim to have honored the classical *ordo* evenly and consistently. For Orthodox and Roman Catholics, preaching has, at least in practice, occupied a less honored position than it has among Protestants. For Protestants, the sacraments have, at least in practice, been pushed to the margins for most of the four-plus centuries that have been dominated by the Enlightenment, even though Luther, Calvin, and later Wesley all believed as firmly as the older traditions that every Lord's Day assembly ought to center on both Word and Sacrament. For Orthodox, Roman, and Protestant traditions, incorporating attentiveness to the poor into the liturgy has been far less consistently focused than it had been in early centuries. "Bath, table, and word," and attentiveness to the poor nevertheless describe the structure of what we might with some caveats call the liturgy, referring to worship in the Sunday assembly, even if it has often been an unrealized ideal in every tradition.

Worship may be genuine when musical genres are eclectic, chosen not so much to represent particular styles as to be appropriate to the occasion and the specific liturgical moment as well as to local cultures; but it may also be genuine even when the music is not so carefully chosen, or even eclectic. The use of various technologies, from print to digital, does not, in and of itself, either guarantee genuineness or deny it. Language, gesture, and movement may vary without compromising the integrity of the liturgy. Worship may occur even if there is no preaching, but a service without it really ought not be described as the liturgy of the church. Worship may occur where there is no Eucharist, but likewise, such a service ought not be described as the liturgy of the church.

Some Christian communities may not care whether their worship is categorized one way or another, and certainly are not required to ask anyone's permission, but for those churches that can trace their origins from the Lutheran, Reformed (Genevan), or Anglican Reformations, it should matter, because a liturgy shaped by what Lathrop calls "bath, table, and word," and attentiveness to the poor is woven into their earliest self-definition as heirs of the apostolic faith. Worship in the Society of Friends (Quakers), the Salvation Army, bodies descended from the so-called Radical Reformation, and Pentecostal churches have different origins and standards. Those communities will make their own cases and speak for themselves, of course. But those churches that claim substantial continuity with the church catholic via one of the Reformations will do well to be attentive to the *ordo* that is both ancient and ecumenical, and measure whether they are realizing it in their own Lord's Day liturgy. When Presbyterian (U.S.A.), United Methodist, United Church of Christ, Episcopal, or Lutheran churches, or their near ecclesiastical kin, choose Lord's Day worship in which either preaching or sacrament is missing, diminished, or only occasional, it is time to recover the catholic heart that beats at the center of these traditions.

Local inculturation of the liturgy of the church ought not extend to separating Word and Sacrament when the assembly gathers on the first day of the week. Preaching once a quarter would be insufficient. Eucharist once a month is insufficient. Local congregations fail to represent their confessional bodies and misrepresent their own identities when they do not hold themselves accountable to the deepest insights of their respective traditions, especially in those matters held in common with the greater church. The same critique may be made of Orthodox and Roman Catholics when they fail to embody with equal vigor each part of the *ordo* of "bath, table, and word," and attentiveness to the poor.

Shaping Worship

Is this demanding too much? If this catholic *ordo* has no authority in the church, then what does? Do churchly habits developed in the centuries during which values of the Enlightenment trumped the values shaped by theological, historical, and biblical standards? Do practices inherited from movements such as Pietism and Puritanism, which came into being as corrections of time- and context-specific weaknesses? If there should be no identifiable standard with which to measure what churches descended from the Lutheran, Reformed, or Anglican Reformations do on Sunday morning, then what is left to help us to shape our worship except to imitate whoever is drawing the largest crowds this year, or to study the "market" in order to cater to current tastes and prejudices? Unfortunately, preference for local inculturation has been misunderstood, and practitioners poorly prepared, and, as a result, the liturgy often becomes distorted. Confusion about mainstream identity and the temptation to take our cues from what passes as expert cultural and generational analysis has taken precedence over liturgical planning that takes seriously history, theology, and the *episkopē* of the chosen officers and teachers of the church.

The value of local inculturation is undermined when worship planners do not know much about the form and contents of the classical *ordo*, treat those whom they wish to attract to worship as consumers whose tastes and distastes take top priority, or do not understand or care that the larger church is also a significant stakeholder in what is done in each assembly on the Lord's Day. Most of today's contemporary Protestant service books have been essentially shaped by the classical liturgies of the church. The services in, for example, *The United Methodist Book of Worship* or *Evangelical Lutheran Worship*, while not identical, are likely to serve as custodians of biblical and theological themes both fashionable and profoundly unfashionable. But all—particularly the unfashionable—are worthy of respectful attention. "For orthodox Christian faith is at the same time the faith of the *church* that is expressed, celebrated, renewed, and, hence, continually constituted in the liturgical assembly as it enacts those very 'holy things' (Lathrop) that the Church *does* in obedience to the biblical command of Christ: 'Do this . . . .'"[5]

Gordon Lathrop's simple outline of the basic moves of the *ordo* ("bath, table, and word," and attention to the poor) allows for a great deal of latitude in fleshing out and performing the liturgy, but it is nevertheless both possible and salutary to have an acquaintance with the contents of classical liturgies sufficiently intimate to be instructed by them, even when—and especially when—there is no chance that they will be used verbatim. For example, in classic liturgies, the Great Thanksgiving, the eucharistic prayer, encapsulates in words as well as actions the faith of the church as it is meant to be embodied in the entire *ordo*. This key prayer developed somewhat differently in early churches that were geographically and sometimes also culturally distant from one another, but as those churches established better means of communicating, the ways they prayed at Eucharist tended to meld into just a few typical forms. The Liturgy of Saint John Chrysostom, the Divine Liturgy of the Byzantine church, is representative of one of those forms: the West Syrian–Byzantine. The West Syrian form has served as the model for contemporary Protestant eucharistic prayers as well as influencing the form of the post–Vatican II Roman Catholic alternatives to the ancient Roman Canon.

Eucharistic Prayer Has Form and Content

The Great Thanksgivings in the newer Protestant service books exemplify the typical West Syrian, Trinitarian, shape—one prayer in three movements.

5. Johnson, *Praying and Believing*, xiii.

The first and second movements are narrative and doxological in style and are framed as thanksgiving, while the third movement is shaped as a petition for the action of the Holy Spirit.

Certain theological/doctrinal themes are typically embedded within each of the three movements. In the first, the assembly, through the voice of the presider, offers thankful praise for God's work in creation and in the history of the covenant people; for the prophets and their witness; for the gift of Jesus Christ; and for specific gifts celebrated on the particular festival day, season, or occasion. The congregation normally responds by singing (or speaking) the Sanctus: an acclamation of praise to the triune God.

The second movement of the eucharistic prayer continues with thanksgivings specifically rooted in narratives of the incarnation, the life and ministry, death, and resurrection of Christ; his ascension and continuing intercession for us; the promise of his coming again; and the gift of the Sacrament, most often including the institution narrative. The congregation again offers a sung or spoken response such as "Christ has died; Christ is risen; Christ will come again."

In the third movement of the prayer, petition takes the place of thanksgiving as the assembly, through the presider, calls upon the Holy Spirit. We pray that the Spirit may bless the assembly and the gifts (bread and cup), making them a participation in Christ's body and blood; that we may be made one with the risen Christ and all God's people, and be united with all the faithful in heaven and on earth; that the Spirit might so nourish us in this Sacrament that we may truly be the body of Christ; that the Spirit might keep us faithful as we turn in ministry toward the world, in anticipation of the promised reign of God (kingdom of God). After an ascription of praise to the triune God, the assembly offers its Amen, sung or spoken. The Lord's Prayer follows.

Ancient eucharistic prayers are long, while contemporary versions are typically less so. The length is not the issue, while both form and contents matter, even when the prayer is shorter and more sharply focused. The tripartite, Trinitarian form carries theological weight. The traditional contents of the prayer ensure that certain biblical and theological themes important to the entire liturgy will not be neglected, as they frequently will be when there is only a Service of the Word, or when the eucharistic prayer is improvised and reduced at the expense of its classic doctrinal content. Seven of the themes most easily lost otherwise include:

- Christ's intercession for us
- the promise of Christ's coming again
- union with Christ and all God's people
- our union with all the faithful in heaven and on earth
- the manifestation of our identity as the body of Christ
- that the church's ministry be directed toward the world
- anticipation of the reign (kingdom) of God

In my experience, all these themes—but particularly the second and the last of the bulleted items, both eschatological in nature—are most likely to be neglected in the absence of the Eucharist or of a classically informed eucharistic prayer. Edwin Chr. van Driel has written that mainstream Protestant churches "need to reclaim the eschatological nature of the gospel. It seems that in the American context our eschatological imagination is either overheated or underdeveloped."[6] These themes are most likely to be underdeveloped in mainstream Protestant churches when there is no eucharistic prayer to lift them up. It is tempting to ignore them because eschatological issues are difficult and challenging; some nonmainline churches have highlighted ("overheated") them to the point of distortion and caricature; and the liturgical local option makes it easy to leave them out, sparing us the challenge they pose. Yet today, at least some quarters of mainstream Protestantism feel drawn to revisit and recover biblical eschatology. Not feverishly predicting the date of an apocalypse, but focusing on the biblical themes of a new creation, a new heaven and earth, and the *basileia* (the reign or kingdom) of God.

The Shape of Eucharistic Prayer Affects the Whole Liturgy

Classical liturgical forms preserve, teach, and model prayer rooted in theological themes that are easily neglected, perhaps even for centuries, but nevertheless have a claim on our attention. Protestants of all stripes have, for too long, focused almost exclusively on questions surrounding personal salvation. No doubt this was a key issue in the conflict between the Protestant reformers and the medieval church: Are we saved by works? By grace? The Apostle Paul, Augustine, and Thomas Aquinas pointed, ultimately, to

---

6. Van Driel, "World is about to Turn," 23.

God's grace, and the reformers echoed them. Contemporary Roman Catholic theologians are likely to do the same, even though they may choose their language carefully. But the Christian hope is not exhausted by questions related to personal salvation, and that is where eschatology comes in. The Christian hope extends further, to the repair and redemption of the entire cosmos, and the affirmation that Christ will be in God's ultimate, cosmic reign and be made manifest as Lord of all. Difficult themes, yes, but compelling ones, too, especially when we are living in an era in which grace versus works draws little existential interest, but the larger questions, where are we headed? and, who (if anyone) is in charge here? are unavoidable.

An example of the contemporary movement to recover in worship the biblical theme of eschatology can be found in *Glory to God*, the new Presbyterian (U.S.A.) hymnal, which devotes two sections to it: "Christ's Return and Judgment," followed by "A New Heaven and Earth," thirty-nine hymns (and Psalm paraphrases) in all.[7] Eschatology is not about pie in the sky by and by, but about ultimate justice: not God getting even and dividing the winners from the losers, but God exorcising, healing, restoring the creation.

Eschatological themes are not the only ones preserved for us in classical eucharistic prayers. Christ's intercession, as represented in the Letter to the Hebrews, and union with Christ and all God's people living now as well as with the faithful departed are deeply biblical themes, easily bypassed when there is no liturgical form that draws our attention to them.

The theological themes threaded throughout classically structured eucharistic prayers are many, and not all have been forgotten. Yet, it is not the place of eucharistic prayer to isolate these themes as though they have no other place in the liturgy, including preaching. The Great Thanksgiving serves as a microcosm of the entire liturgy. Those who use the Revised Common Lectionary will encounter specific biblical texts that ground all these themes, including eschatology, and if the preacher is brave enough to accept the challenge of dealing with them head-on, both the preacher and the congregation will likely discover something rich and beautiful.

Classically shaped eucharistic prayers (Great Thanksgivings) ensure that grateful praise occupies a central place in the liturgy of the assembly. The Christian life is meant to nurture the ability to offer thanks and encourage us to learn how to provide mutual support when being thankful is hard. Thankfulness is not a mood, nor is it produced by an effort to think

---

7. Presbyterian Church (U.S.A.), *Glory to God*.

positively, but rather derives from nurturing the hope that rests in God. The aim is to cultivate the gift of thankfulness even in times of bitter disappointment, not only for good things past and or even present, but also for the good that lies ahead, secured by God's promise of a new creation, represented in the resurrection of the Lord.

Thanksgiving can be restrained and even elusive in some eucharistic practice, particularly where the Sacrament is construed as a replay of the Last Supper, a melancholy final meal focused only on the betrayal and death of Christ, with little regard for the resurrection. The Last Supper is not the only meal that shapes the church's Eucharist. All the biblical meals serve as witnesses to the multidimensional meanings of the Sacrament, including Old Testament meals eaten "in the presence of God," Jesus's meals with sinners, the meals involved in the feedings of the multitudes, postresurrection meals, and eschatological meals.[8] Arguably, the first Lord's Supper in the New Testament is represented in the account from Luke 24 of the two bewildered disciples on the Emmaus road who recognize the risen Lord when he sits with them and breaks bread at the table. The Sacrament is not a painful revisiting of a time of sad farewell but a joyful feast, the host of which is the One who died but has risen, the One whose resurrection serves to point ahead to the ultimate rebirth of the whole creation.

The Liturgical Use of Creeds

The Apostles' and Nicene Creeds were used primarily in catechesis or in baptisms until the Nicene Creed came into use in the eucharistic liturgy "in the sixth century at Constantinople and in the eleventh at Rome."[9] To profess the creed together is a doxological act and has value even though the eucharistic prayer rehearses similar themes, because saying or singing the creed imprints it upon the memory more effectively than simply hearing it. Some mainstream Protestant congregations are accustomed to the liturgical use of an ecumenical creed, while others are not; and certainly mid-American generic Protestantism does not welcome their use, though they may substitute affirmations that seem more culturally acceptable. Even in congregations in which one of the ecumenical creeds is commonly used, some members object to it because they disagree with or don't understand

8. Byars, *Sacraments*.
9. Johnson, *Praying and Believing*, 131.

a line, a phrase, or the whole thing, and, in the interest of personal integrity, think it improper to join in.

Here again we encounter the problem of a profound misunderstanding of what liturgy is and does. In a cultural framework shaped by the dominant paradigms of rationalism and individualism, fueled by what remains of Pietism and Puritanism, it seems as though the Lord's Day assembly is meant to be primarily a gathering of individuals whose beliefs are expected to match closely enough that all can honorably coordinate their private devotions for an hour or so. What is missing in this view of public worship is that a congregation is more than the sum of its parts. A congregation consists of those whom, in baptism, God has called together, uniting them with Christ and one another and the whole communion of saints on earth and in heaven. It is the assembly of those whom God has given an identity as a manifestation of the body of Christ in a particular place.

The body of Christ, like any other sort of body, is made up of diverse parts. In the case of the worshiping congregation, it includes the very young and the very old, those experienced in the church's life and worship along with the inexperienced, those who process language well and those who don't, those who have explored spiritual things in depth and those who have not, those who engage the world primarily with the intellect and those who engage primarily through one or more of the senses. What the assembled congregation does, despite individual differences, it does as an ensemble. To shape what is done in the worshiping assembly as though it needs to be an expression of each individual's faith as expressed personally and uniquely would be either to fall into chaos (as much as though all should be speaking in tongues), or to create a sequence of events so innocuous as to offend no one. If worship means anything, then the various persons present in the assembly will encounter in diverse ways and with various responses not just the creed but also prayers, hymns, sacraments, and preaching. What is deeply meaningful to one will be challenging or puzzling to another.

The creed is the creed *of the church*, which is to say that while you or I would likely express our personal faith in language of our own devising, the creed is both an affirmation of the body as a whole and a means by which members of the assembly engage with the faith of the church. The creed is the voice of the church, inclusive of those near and far, living and dead, articulate and inarticulate. It is both unrealistic and unnecessary to imagine that everyone will affirm the creed with the same degree of understanding and confidence, or even that a particular member of the church will affirm the creed in the same way this week as she will next week. To affirm the creed is a communal act, and to participate in it as a communal act is part of a lifelong process of pondering the central affirmations of the faith and growing into them. The creeds are embodiments of the affirmations with which we in the church have to do. What puzzles or seems off-putting at one stage of life may astonish by its relevance at a later date, and fill in a blank at still another stage. To presume that a member of the body must understand the creed just exactly so, right now, or else refuse to add one's voice to the body's communal affirmation, profoundly misunderstands the role of the creed in liturgy and in spiritual formation.

Perhaps it is saying of the creed rather than singing it (at least occasionally) that is part of the problem. In our Enlightenment-shaped culture, to say something implies that we fully understand what we are saying, that we endorse it, that we stand behind it personally. Curiously, those presumptions don't apply when we sing a hymn or chorus. Were we to say the words of a hymn aloud, without music, we might be as puzzled or resistant as we may be when we say the creed. Singing a text somehow signals that the language is to be understood similarly to the way one understands poetry. In other words, sung language is clearly not meant to be as tightly precise as an invoice or as the transcript of an eyewitness's testimony in court. One intuitively knows that a sung text engages the heart and the imagination, and the heart has its own grammar. When a congregation sings a hymn or psalm, they do not generally feel compelled to decode and question it line by line, but instinctively join in the communal act of offering it to God on behalf of all. No wonder, then, that so often in history the creed has been chanted or sung as a doxological act by Orthodox, Catholics, and Protestants, including by the sixteenth-century reforming churches.

The Theological Architecture of the Liturgy

The mistaken notion that every individual present in the assembly must understand the creed and personally endorse it before joining in the communal affirmation is matched by a similar misperception that it is necessary to understand prayer and how it "works" before praying. Prayer is not a tool that can be utilized to fix problems on demand, even though our prayer may become more intense when we are focused on a problem, whether personal or universal. In common prayer, we lay before God our own concerns and the needs of neighbors, near and far. Prayer turns our attention toward those whom we might otherwise ignore or turn away from. Our praying also serves to deepen and focus our reliance on God, who may help us to see our own duties more clearly, but also assure us that even when our imagination fails and our strength to make things right are limited, God is at work in ways that we cannot precisely track or measure. In short, we pray because our instincts lead us to pray, even when we cannot explain it in a way that would be scientifically acceptable. To believe in God is to learn to trust God, and to trust God is to reach out to God, and so we pray, leaving the mystery of it in God's own hands, relinquishing any claim that we control God, or might control God if we could get prayer all figured out.

The liturgy of the church in Word and Sacrament, with attentiveness to the poor, shapes the disposition of worshipers over time and imprints on them the architectural structure that supports personal and communal engagement with the God revealed in the gospel of Jesus Christ. The liturgy functions as a sort of holistic, gestalt encounter with the story of God's reaching out to humankind, especially in and with Israel, and in Jesus Christ crucified, risen, ascended, whose coming in glory we anticipate. The liturgy has a teaching function, but not in a classroom sense. The liturgy of the church is at work both in the conscious and the unconscious mind. It works through sound and speech, but also in bodily movement, as well as by means of the senses, such as sight, smell, and taste. But for it to be coherent, those who are new to the community need to learn how to trace the contours of the biblical story that is embodied in the liturgy of the church.

Preaching is first and foremost a sacramental act, but it also functions as a means of modeling the ways that language is used in the church. With the word *language* I don't mean simply defining biblical or ecclesiastical in-words. I also mean providing models for encountering the triune God in and between the lines of nuanced, multifaceted language; I mean showing how it functions in simile and metaphor along with discursive uses. This is the preacher's challenge, whether it has been thought through in those terms or not. For example, what might grace look like for someone trembling before the challenge of middle school, or for persons whose child has broken their hearts? What might resurrection mean for those who lament the manifest injustices of this world, both social and personal? There is more than one way to understand symbolic uses of such biblical words as *water, wine, bread, sight, light, death,* and *life*. Preaching that seriously engages biblical texts recognizes that the gospel story is told using "metaphors and stories intertextually linked in reinterpretive chains."[10] Metaphors and similes may be innovative, but are not infinitely so. Whether in Scripture, liturgical language, or preaching, they are anchored in a context that revolves around the specificity of a particular God, revealed in Christ, whose Holy Spirit is at work in the church and the world.

Mentoring

For those being exposed to the faith of the church for the first time, or beginning a process of relearning the faith after a bad experience with some version of it, the church's goal might be to help to instill a healthy piety. Can the word *piety* be reclaimed? In today's culture, to call someone pious is an insult, since the word and its variants is typically taken to mean "smug," "complacent," and "self-righteous." Whether or not we may discover some alternative word that conveys the original, positive intent of the word *piety*, to embrace the gospel is always more than giving intellectual assent. The Christian life does have to do with a particular story, and with doctrinal content that interprets the meaning of the story, but it is also a way of being positioned in the world. After Vatican II, the Roman Catholic Church instituted a catechumenal process called RCIA, or Rite of Christian Initiation for Adults. Other churches, including Episcopalians, ELCA Lutherans, United Methodists, and Mennonites, have created their own versions of the RCIA. The contemporary catechumenate takes for its model similar processes for socializing new Christians in faith as those that the church used at about the time it rose to imperial favor in the era of Constantine. Persons who respond to an invitation to enter a formal catechumenate, or some variation on it, undertake a spiritual apprenticeship intended to nurture their personal faith under the stewardship of the church, whose calling is to teach, practice, and exhibit the faith it has received.

A catechumenal process is just that: socializing new Christians into the ways the faith is believed and practiced. How do we engage with Scripture? How do we think theologically? How do we pray? How do we use personal and communal resources in a responsible way as disciples of Jesus Christ? Where and how might one find a place in personal and communal ministries of service? The various catechumenates are not clergy-centered but depend on lay members of congregations to serve as mentors to those who are exploring faith as it is practiced in and by the church. To set up a

---

10. Lathrop, *Four Gospels*, 203.

catechumenal process is a challenge, because it requires identifying church members who have the gifts to serve as mentors, whether for a group or one-on-one. After years of leaving formation in the faith to a few years of voluntary attendance at Sunday school and youth groups, and more or less presuming that parents will form their own children in the faith, or that the culture at large will do it for them, not every congregation will find it easy to identify people willing and able to serve in a catechumenal ministry. This dilemma is the unfortunate legacy of several American centuries when the church enjoyed such status in the larger culture that it felt little pressure to update ways of forming people in the stories, the doctrinal content, or the practice of the Christian faith. The result is today's situation, in which the mainstream church in particular finds itself pretty much disarmed when and if it becomes aware of the need to support much more intentional formation.

What are pastors to do when they look out upon congregations they love, seeing people with many talents and virtues, but can identify only a few who might serve as mentors in the faith? One thing they might do is to start with those who hold office in the congregation: elders, deacons, trustees, official boards, congregation councils, sessions, vestries, consistories. These bodies both resemble and differ from secular boards that govern both for-profits and nonprofits. Administrative church bodies resemble secular administrative bodies in the sense that in their given arena, these bodies have, of necessity, to do with mundane affairs such as money (income and expenditures), personnel matters, upkeep and improvement of infrastructure, and the like. Church administrative bodies differ from secular boards in that they are ecclesiastical structures—bodies charged with carrying out tasks related to God, God's call, and the building up of the body of Christ. Therefore, they are also praying bodies—groups of officers whose responsibility includes the duty and delight of learning how to think theologically about their charge. A pastor's challenge is to help these various governing councils understand how their corporate identity differs from secular equivalents, and to lead them to dedicate meeting time that includes common prayer, mutual support, and exploring ways of thinking theologically even about budgets and the stewardship of buildings and property. When service as a church officer becomes a spiritually rich experience, those who have served become a vital source from which to identify and recruit potential mentors with resources useful for nurturing newcomers and others in Christian faith and practice.

Active participation in the liturgy of the church, a goal important both to the Protestant reformers and the reforms of the Second Vatican Council, is more than a matter of joining one's voice with the voices of the congregation, as valuable as that is. It is also a matter of acquiring skills to discern how the liturgy leads to deeper engagement with the gospel story, and most particularly, engagement with the Lord of the gospel. Such engagement includes use of the intellect—knowing the story—but it also involves *sensing* the story: intuiting it in all its simplicity and complexity, an intuiting supported by bodily as well as intellectual engagement. Such intuition differs among individuals and in the various seasons of our lives but is always supported by and linked to the liturgy of Word and Sacrament. A mentoring process for formation in the faith, whether it takes the form of a formal catechumenate or not, plays a key role in helping to integrate a cognitive understanding of the church's faith with a personal, existential commitment to it nurtured by the liturgy and the biblical and theological affirmations that it embodies. Such commitment is expressed both as personal piety and as courage for living as Christ's disciples in the world.

Local Inculturation Revisited

Although local inculturation represents a potentially significant value for Christian worship, it is one that has not served many Protestants as well as it might, simply because such inculturation cannot be implemented as effortlessly as it may seem. The point is, after all, that it is the liturgy of the *church* that is meant to be made manifest in local cultures, and to do that requires those who are responsible for implementing it to understand classical liturgies well enough in both form and content to be able to recognize what is essential to its integrity and how that might be realized liturgically in culturally appropriate ways. To do that competently is much more difficult than to use an established liturgy verbatim. The discernment necessary to do it successfully is not just a matter for those versed in liturgy, but also and especially requires theological skills of the sort that those who have experienced a seminary education ought reasonably be expected to have acquired. And yet, it is more typically the case that even those who have studied theology as part of their academic training are at a loss when it comes to perceiving its relation to the church's worship. Particularly difficult is the work of identifying those theological essentials that are missing from the typical liturgical diets of worshiping assemblies whose primary experience has been local option.

It is one thing to analyze the meaning of this or that rite, or moment in a rite, when it is familiar and well-known to worshipers, and quite another to be able to take note of deeply important theological themes that are typically either entirely absent, or present but severely truncated. For example, if established local custom includes confession and pardon in a liturgy, it is possible to identify there the theological themes of penitence and forgiveness, but when there is no confession and pardon, those who plan or evaluate the liturgy in that place may simply overlook what is not there to be evaluated. Eschatological themes represent another example of more than average importance. When eschatological themes are absent from the liturgy, as they usually are, it is not a matter of the liturgy losing something marginal and exotic, but of losing nothing less than the entire panoramic view of the Christian hope as rooted in the gospel of Jesus Christ, crucified and risen. To lose the eschatological horizon particularly has the effect of deforming the Eucharist, depriving it of its eyes-forward momentum, with the result that it confuses the liturgical action as a whole, from beginning to end.

James K. A. Smith notes, "Liturgies are formative . . . Liturgies are covert incubators of the imagination . . . Liturgies traffic in the dynamics of metaphor and narrative and drama as performed pictures of the good life, staged performances of some vision of the kingdom that capture our imagination and thus orient our love and longing."[11] A liturgy sufficiently attuned to classic biblical and theological themes, whether familiar or long neglected, serves as an essential anchor to ground Protestants today in the faith of the church. True, Christians in the twenty-first century may understand eschatological hope differently than Christians in the first century or the nineteenth, but it is the same hope, and because it is the same hope, it is the same faith. Christians today may understand eschatological hope differently from one another, but even so, this is one of those substantial things with which Christian faith has to do: Different views, varied perspectives, diverse ways of dealing with it, but the same faith. The same can be said for other neglected affirmations preserved in classical liturgical forms, whether Christ's intercession for us (for example); or our union with all the faithful in heaven and on earth; or the church's identity as "royal priesthood," intercessors and advocates for the world. To the extent that

---

11. Smith, *Imagining*, 137.

such themes either are unfamiliar or, worse, seem irrelevant in a world as needy as ours feels now, the church has lost a pearl of great price, and the cost for such a loss is high.

The faith of the church (expressed as theology) has provided shape, form, and substance to its liturgy. In return, the church's liturgy serves as a means with which to embody and hand on that faith in a form of rite and prayer that affirms the theological identity of the triune God who is both subject and object of our faith, and whose identity reveals our identity as the church. For those for whom the catholicity of the church is a positive to be embraced, classically informed liturgy embodied in Word and Sacrament is indispensable, whether texts are used strictly from the book, or as a source and model to serve as guide in adapting the classic liturgy to local norms. While such a liturgy not only permits local inculturation but may be the richer for it, it is a fact nevertheless that Protestants today need to wrestle with the downside of having sacrificed so much liturgical authority to local options. The inevitable losses have an impact on every aspect of the church's life—not only its worship.

For some generations the quality (real or perceived) of preaching compensated for the hollowness of the liturgy of some mainstream Protestant churches, but that day is over. In a wired world, preaching faces formidable competition, and yet frequently it is the case that those whose responsibility it is to preach seem not to be aware of how much attention and imagination is required to preach in today's cultural situation—not to mention how much courage it takes. Preaching in the twenty-first century requires reimagining today's congregation, which, though many of its members have been worshiping for many years, does not hear either Scripture or sermon in the same way the same people heard them as recently as a decade or two ago. When crafted with sensitivity to the text and to the listeners, preaching still has the capacity to exert enormous power and exercise substantial authority, but it can carry only half the weight required. We live in an era attuned to the multisensory, a perfect opening for the rediscovery of the rich possibilities of the sacramental dimensions of preaching and worship.

Having benefited by a self-replicating, socially privileged existence more or less successfully for generations, with a constituency we imagined we could count on, we Protestants have outlived the relevance of parts of the Protestant ethos that evolved to suit very different circumstances, now changed nearly beyond recognition. Turning away from reflexive but not always reflective habits of thought and practice is not to become less

Protestant, but to rediscover the catholicity that beats even at the heart of the Reformation and is our heritage to cherish and to provide support as we reposition ourselves in a new cultural climate.

The Church

In the U.S., anybody can start a church. It requires no denominational blessing, no district superintendent, no bishop, no presbytery, no synod or annual conference, and no need to report to the government beyond incorporating and establishing tax-exempt status. It happens all the time. Entrepreneurs, some of them charismatic (in the broad sense of the word) or otherwise gifted, start their own churches and, in effect, run them exactly as they see fit, not obligated to report to anyone. Often such start-ups have grown into megachurches, sometimes meeting in multiple sites. The faith to which such congregations are exposed is the faith of the pastor. Preaching, worship, and teaching will be measured by the scope, depth, and breadth of the pastor's personal knowledge and vision, filtered through the pastor's personality. And so it is that the proliferation of denominations has been joined by the phenomenon of multiple independent congregations neither obligated nor connected to any other, and feeling no responsibility to the greater church, its defining landmarks, or its faith.

Mid-American generic Protestantism has contributed to this phenomenon, however unintentionally, because it has tended to understand the church as a useful option, capable of being helpful to individuals in the cultivation of their personal faith, but otherwise something to take or leave. According to popular lore, what matters is only the Bible, personal religious experience, and living a moral and ethical life. But that is a naïve point of view. The Bible has been and still is received and handed on, but by whom? The Bible is handed on by the church, whose book it is. Personal religious experience is almost meaninglessly generic, without any words to report it or make sense of it apart from the communal language that has grown out of the experience of some community, whether the community of Buddhists or humanists or the church. However personal the Bible reading or the religious experience may be, no one becomes a Christian without having been touched by the church, whether one realizes it or not.

The church, in fact, is not an optional add-on but part of the gospel. To be united with Christ in baptism is to be united with his church. It is the mentor that coaches us in how to talk the talk and walk the walk. It is the milieu in which we practice meeting the difficult challenges of the gospel, including learning how to live in community with people we have not personally selected as our companions in faith. It is a shared life—both difficult and nurturing—that enables us to see and experience how what seems to be a random cross-section of the human race might actually be a manifestation of the body of Christ, exercising a corporate priesthood to the world.

Where there is reasonable and effective *episkopē* to guard the health of the body, such oversight provides safeguards intended to support the integrity of the faith the church has received and of which it serves as a responsible steward. That is a faith richer and more diverse than many may imagine, but not an inchoate collection of millions of separate, contending, and unrelated opinions or spiritual insights bundled together. There is your faith and mine, but all within a larger context—the faith *of the church*.

And that's what is at stake on Sunday morning: nothing less than the faith of the church. Not faith in general, or even personal faith, but *the church's* faith, as represented and traditioned in and through the defining landmarks with which the church always has to do. American mainstream Protestants have arrived at a *kairos* moment—a moment for repositioning: letting go of some things in order to establish a firmer grip on others, some of which we have too hastily, in the passion of specific historical conflicts, abandoned. It is time to open the boxes we have hidden away with the jumble in the attic, and to unwrap the gifts that God has provided for us from the very beginning, claiming as our own those treasures intended for the whole body—particularly, the treasures of Word and Sacrament, in all their fullness, along with attentiveness to the poor.

5

Attentiveness to the Poor
Revisiting the Protestant Ethic

A Liturgical Basic

REPOSITIONING OURSELVES SOMETIMES INVOLVES stepping back to get a better theological perspective on things we already believe and are already practicing: reframing them as we enter a new era. Gordon Lathrop describes the basic liturgy of the church in the simplest terms possible: bath, book, meal, and attentiveness to the poor. Concern for the vulnerable and needy is deeply rooted in the ministry of Jesus and the early church, building on many precedents in the Old Testament. When the Apostle Paul met with the leaders of the Jerusalem church and received their blessing and acknowledgement of his calling to minister to the Gentiles, "they asked only one thing, that we remember the poor, which was actually what I was eager to do" (Gal 2:10). Paul asked Christians in distant, largely Gentile outposts to collect money to be shared with "the poor among the saints at Jerusalem" (Rom 15:16). As Luke records it in his account of the early church, those Christians who had access to resources sold them and brought the proceeds to the apostles, "and it was distributed to each as any had need" (Acts 4:35).

While the church from earliest memory had made provision to gather offerings for the needs of the poor, it was only gradually that such offerings began to be incorporated into the actions of the liturgy. In about the middle of the second century, Justin, an early Christian martyr, wrote in his *First*

Apology a description of the Lord's Day liturgy in Rome. Justin had traveled widely, and it is likely that his observations about the weekly assembly in Rome would apply as well to his experience with churches elsewhere. He describes a liturgy of the Word and Eucharist, remarking that, after the eucharistic prayer,

> There is a distribution of the things over which thanks have been said and each person participates, and these things are sent by the deacons to those who are not present. Those who are prosperous and who desire to do so, give what they wish, according to each one's own choice, and the collection is deposited with the presider. He aids orphans and widows, those who are in want through disease or through another cause, those who are in prison, and foreigners who are sojourning here. In short, the presider is a guardian to all those who are in need.[1]

Lathrop suggests that Christian practice in Justin's time may reflect an early reform that took place in response to Paul's rebuke of the Corinthians for ignoring the poor while others ate their fill at the assembly's communal meal (1 Corinthians 11:21–22). "Now the juxtaposition of word and meal ritual inevitably involves a third focus: the poor."[2]

Concern for the poor is intimately related to the Eucharist. In the middle of the third century, according to Jungmann, Bishop Cyprian scolded "a rich woman for her lack of charity in failing to bring a gift. Apparently the individual worshiper was bound not only to contribute to the community poor box (*corban*) but also to make an offering for the altar, and from Cyprian's words it is quite clear that this offering was nothing more nor less than the bread and wine."[3]

Practices varied. In some places, worshipers brought bread and wine from their own homes and set them in a specially designated place before the beginning of the service. At the beginning of the eucharistic action, deacons took from these gifts enough for use in the Eucharist and presented them to the presider, while after the service the unclaimed surplus would be distributed to those who needed it for sustenance. In other places, the faithful took their gifts directly to the altar or table themselves. What we today call the offertory has its origin in the ceremonial procession in which the people or designated officers carried bread and wine to the altar

---

1. Lathrop, *Holy Things*, 45.
2. Ibid., 46.
3. Jungmann, *Mass of the Roman Catholic Rite*, 316.

or table for use in the eucharistic meal, but clearly, in its origin, all of these ceremonial actions were closely linked to a conscious intention of providing for those in need. Indeed, the communal life of the church from earliest times associated assembling for Word and Sacrament with coordinating practical help for the poor.

Ron Luckey, a pastor in the Evangelical Lutheran Church in America (ELCA), reports that on his first trip to Ranquitte, Haiti, "I worshipped at St. Francis of Assisi Roman Catholic Church. The offering consisted of some money but, along with bread and wine, baskets and tin pots of mango, corn, sugar cane, beans, rice, etc. This was brought in procession to the altar by those who had grown these crops in their little plots of land. The priest told me that he and some helpers would be taking this food 'from the poor' into the hills to distribute to 'the poorest of the poorest of the poor.' How Justinian!"[4]

The Theological, Liturgical Point of an Offering

The Protestant reformers continued the ancient practice of collecting alms for the poor, although methods of doing this varied considerably. Neither the early Lutherans nor Reformed nor Anglicans continued the tradition of an offertory procession of the bread and wine, but all made provision for collecting money for the poor either within the service or at the door after the service had concluded. Practice varied from time to time and place to place, in each tradition. In Calvin's Geneva, it was the special responsibility of the deacons to encourage the faithful to provide for the needy, usually at the door as the congregation exited the service. In England, the first Book of Common Prayer (1549) left the offertory in place at the beginning of the Anglican eucharistic liturgy, but the tone was altered substantially. The procession of the gifts of bread and wine was abandoned, and sentences related to almsgiving were added: "The people presented their money, not at the altar, but into a chest, which was placed in the choir."[5] The second prayer book made further changes: the church wardens collected the people's alms and deposited them into "the poremens boxe."[6] In John Wesley's *Sunday Service*, the elder presiding read passages of Scripture while someone

---

4. Pastor Ron Luckey, in a personal e-mail to the author, May 23, 2014.
5. Thompson, *Liturgies*, 234.
6. Ibid., 241.

appointed for the purpose passed "a decent Bason" to collect the people's alms, then presented it to the elder who placed it upon the Table.[7]

While the practice of collecting the people's financial gifts has persisted through the centuries and even until today, it has become less and less clearly associated with "attentiveness to the poor." Most of those visiting a church for the first time will have little notion of what happens to the money worshipers are placing in the offering plate. An international student confided that, on his first visit to a Christian church, he presumed that money was being collected for the pastor! In a sense, that is not an entirely unreasonable presumption, since the gifts in the plate go, ordinarily, to fund the church budget, which includes payment of staff salaries as well as utility bills, building maintenance, and the like. Some portion is normally designated for mission or benevolences, which includes denominational causes as well as institutions and projects that the congregation has specifically chosen to support. It is possible to make the case that the funding of all this is, in fact, mission, whether money pays utility bills or purchases a computer for the office or goes to the local soup kitchen or homeless shelter—and no doubt that is true. And yet, because the checks and bills deposited in the plate go to support a budget, the identity of those who are being served by the offerings is abstract and even obscure. Many have only a hazy idea of how the money is spent. Maybe that is why one may occasionally hear a church member talk about "paying my dues."

In the church where I worship, most pledging members write a check to the church once a month, and it is frequently the case in congregations that people are making their contributions online, using a credit card. Actual cash in the offering plate on most Sundays is likely to come from visitors and others who attend only occasionally, although in many "seeker-friendly" services, the presiding officer announces that visitors are not expected to take part in the offering at all, that being one of the responsibilities of church members. As the actual collection of checks and money as a liturgical act on the Lord's Day is becoming less likely to be the conduit by which church members normally support the congregation and its outreach, the offering seems increasingly distant from its liturgical role as an embodied act signaling the church's concern for the poor.

---

7. Ibid., 426.

The Eucharistic Link

Just as "attentiveness to the poor" has become muted in the liturgy itself, it has frequently lost its eucharistic connection. In those congregations that celebrate the Eucharist only occasionally rather than every week, the offering remains part of the liturgy even though the absence of Eucharist breaks the integral relationship between the two. From early times on, the relationship was evident: we bring food, we are fed, we give food away. One can justify an offering even when it does not lead to its intended end, the Eucharist, but something is lost in the separation of the two. One scholar has noted that "apart from feeding the hungry, the Eucharist becomes a ritual detached from life, just as feeding the hungry, apart from the Eucharist, is not fully satisfying."[8]

As Protestants reposition ourselves, one that deserves serious attention is the recovery of this deeply rooted but frequently forgotten relationship between the church's liturgy of word and meal, on the one hand, and care for the poor on the other. One suggestion, made by Lathrop, is "the recovery of the use of the Sunday collection primarily or even only for the poor."[9] Yes, of course such a change in practice would certainly require a program of reeducating the congregation, and no doubt the people on the finance committee and the governing council would be nervous, even resistant. But what an opportunity such a change offers to explore with both officers and congregation biblical roots of the church's liturgical practice. What an opportunity to heighten the sense of the church's identity and mission as a community whose work is, among other things, to give food away!

Pledged money to fund the ministries of the local congregation (including budgeted causes designated for mission and outreach) could be collected otherwise, just as is often the case already, while financial gifts collected during the service could be exclusively for the soup kitchen, for the homeless shelter, for refugees and victims of natural disasters, for a hospital or educational institution run by mission workers, or for the denomination. Then the Sunday offering would rise above the level of abstraction, since it would be easy to make clear that these monies are not collected for our use but for others.

The sense that the church's liturgy is and ought to be intimately related to "attentiveness to the poor" has theological as well as ethical implications

---

8. Craddock, *Luke*, 126.
9. Lathrop, *Holy Things*, 156.

and, in fact, is bound up with the basic identity of the church and its purpose in the world. Is the church simply another benevolent institution, like one of the several service clubs, whose aim is to do some good in the community? Is it an association for those who, embracing the wisdom of the gospel, are somehow in the know (i.e., gnostics), giving them a significant advantage over their neighbors who don't know the score? Is the church a group of people whom God favors with perks, privileges, and status not available to everyone else? Is it the company of those who can count on being heaven bound? Or, more simply, is the church best described as an institution whose purpose is to provide a sense of community as well as a variety of services for those who belong to it?

My impression is that members of mainline churches are likely to believe, whether explicitly or implicitly, that the church justifies its existence with one or another of these several ways of describing the church's identity and purpose in the world, even though the ones that are not false are inadequate. As long as people keep participating in the life of the church, it may seem that it need not matter much to its leadership whether the faithful have a clear picture of what sort of community the church is meant to be, or of what purpose it is intended to serve, but it does matter. And one reason it matters is especially evident as we consider the calling to be attentive to the poor.

The Church as a Priestly People

To the extent that Protestants have adapted to the ideology of the Enlightenment, they have increasingly focused on the individual's personal faith and piety, as though the communal identity of the church should take second place, if it deserves any place at all. And yet, the New Testament writers were writing, first of all, for the community—the church—rather than for individuals. While individuals will, of course, hear themselves addressed in the Scriptures, the fact that the Bible is intended for a community—a people—is inescapable. The first letter of Peter provides a clue to the identity and purpose of the church, and that identity and purpose is something other than a random association of individuals working on their spirituality together or coordinating their good works. The writer addresses the church, saying, "But you are a chosen race, a royal priesthood, a holy nation" (1 Peter 2:9).

That word *chosen* may be troubling, because it seems to imply special privilege and, of course, the word has often been flung back at the Jews in resentment when non-Jews have misunderstood it as though it were a claim to superiority. Equally, *priesthood* is a word that doesn't sound very Protestant. It helps us to understand these images better if we explore their roots in the Old Testament. When God called Abraham and Sarah, God promised that they would become the progenitors of a great nation, "and in you all the families of the earth shall be blessed" (Genesis 12:3). Why this people among all the peoples should have been chosen is a mystery, and clearly it has brought them both blessing and grief. But whatever *chosen* means, it clearly implies that they have a vocation directed toward the blessing of "all the families of the earth." As for that alien word *priesthood*, we may understand it better in the light of God's declaration that Moses was directed to pass on to the whole people of Israel: "But you shall be for me a priestly kingdom and a holy nation" (Exodus 19:6).

"Chosen" and "priesthood" are two ways of describing the same identity and purpose, and "holy nation," found in both the Exodus 19 and the 1 Peter 2 passages, provides a further definition. Through Jesus Christ, God has called out the church and given it a corporate identity and purpose that it shares with Israel, one that involves a special vocation to be a community, a "holy nation," whose ultimate aim and purpose is to be a "blessing" to "all the families of the earth." A community that shares a communal priesthood is one that does priestly work.

And what is priestly work? It is here, I'm afraid, that the traditional Protestant celebration of the priesthood of all believers has gone astray. As formulated in the Reformation, the doctrine of the priesthood of all believers was meant as a critique of the idea that salvation was impossible without the mediation of a caste of specific officers ordained to the priesthood. Well and good. However, the doctrine accumulated other, less worthy interpretations, usually by identifying priesthood as a task for individual Christians rather than for the church as a whole. For example, it began to be understood as the idea that none of us needs help from anybody else—neither intercession nor advocacy. With God, we are our own priests, and so we can manage on our own. That notion squares nicely with Enlightenment individualism but is out of touch with reality and hardly biblical.

A second way of misunderstanding the doctrine is to imagine that it means that the church has no need to distinguish any roles or offices, as though every Christian is functionally interchangeable with every other.

This is certainly a radically democratic idea, but it is neither realistic nor biblical (cf. 1 Corinthians 12).

A third way of misunderstanding the priesthood of all believers is to understand the doctrine as affirming God's call to each of the faithful to be priests to one another. That rings true and is certainly consistent with Scripture, but a broader understanding of the biblical understanding of the church's calling to be "a royal priesthood" is that God has chosen and commissioned the body as a whole to exercise a corporate priestly ministry to the whole world. And what does such a priestly ministry look like?

Job Description for a Priestly People

A priest is both an intercessor and an advocate. The Letter to the Hebrews supplies a metaphorical image of Jesus as "high priest," and Christians are "holy partners in a heavenly calling" (Hebrews 3:1). The church's corporate, priestly identity and purpose is to intercede—to pray for and be an advocate for those who need an intercessor and advocate. Those with such a need are the vulnerable—the contemporary equivalents of widows and orphans—and certainly the poor, the voiceless, those who have no power in the world.

If the leadership of a congregation were to facilitate a conversation beginning with the question of why we have an offering in our Lord's Day service, exploring its biblical origins, and asking what purposes it is meant to serve; then if the leadership were to invite consideration of devoting the monies raised in the offertory rite exclusively to serving only those causes specifically designated for the support, service, and needs of others, we would be moving toward a discussion of what the church's basic identity and purpose might be. Then we could talk about what it means for God to have chosen, or called, a people to share the delights and burdens of following Christ as he leads us to find ways of facilitating the blessing of "all the families of the earth," which is to say, lots of people who may or may not be part of our church or any other. That would be a conversation worth having, and one that might not be completed in an evening or in a Lenten series, but that might continue to bear fruitful results for years.

If Protestant mainstream churches could be led to leave behind the sort of definitions of identity and purpose usually shaped by the model of the marketplace, in which churches compete with others for constituents, money, and influence, it could spark a renaissance, a rebirth. Not necessarily one measured by an increase in numbers or favorable attention, but a renaissance even more important than that, anchored in a general awakening to the identity given us in Christ. Who are we? We are those whom God has called together not only for our own sake but to seek a blessing for those easily forgotten and neglected or identified as competitors or even enemies. What would it be like if every member of the church understood herself to have been called to share in a communal priesthood, rooted in God's act of joining her to Christ in baptism? How might that shape the way we think about baptism, the way we position our fonts and baptisteries, the way we enable people upon entering the place of worship to see and reflect upon the sacrament that joins us together in royal priesthood? How might the aim of sharing in a communal priesthood to seek the blessing of "all the families of the earth" shape the conversations in church councils and boards, committees and task forces, choirs and youth groups, classes, small groups, and groups designed to mentor inquirers, as well as ecclesiastical bodies beyond the local parish?

Founded on and nourished by bath, book, and meal, "attentiveness to the poor" is not just a duty or an obligation, but it is, paradoxically and at the same time, God's gift to us of a holy participation in a shared identity and purpose, one that kindles our imagination and energies as we try to discover what "blessing" might look like in this or that place, for these people or those, in the neighborhood or far away, though within God's reach and often our own. Who are we? We are, collectively, a "royal priesthood." And "the poor" certainly may be defined in broad strokes, to include all sorts of people who are in one way or another in need of a helping hand, vulnerable, or at risk.

Intercession Matters

A priest intercedes, commends to God those who need help. As one who has been sitting in the pew for a few years, I can testify to the fact that intercessory prayer matters to people in congregations, whatever it may mean to those for whom the prayers have been offered. In times of wars and pressure to make or intervene in wars, in times when suicide bombings and mass murders in schools or theaters or malls are no longer surprising enough to make the front pages, in an era when governing is stymied by partisan standoffs, when political campaigning never stops between elections, and when whoever has the most money calls the shots, it is sometimes all one can do to get out of bed in the morning. Before church, the newspaper or the radio delivers enough bad news for a week, or you log on to a website that ignites righteous indignation sufficient to curdle the cream in your morning coffee. Then, it's off to worship. My expectation is not that the one who preaches will explain it all to us, diagnose the problems in the news and announce a prescription for what ails us, but that we might be led, through the voice of the one leading us in prayer, to lay before God the suffering of refugees; the falling of governments; the victims of droughts and hurricanes, tornados and floods. When such intercessions are actually made, it doesn't reduce my responsibility to be concerned or even to find concrete ways of expressing my concern, but it does take the edge off the bitterness and hopelessness that can so easily descend into a sense of helplessness. In this simple way, praying our intercessions, we are taking the first step of actualizing our vocation to be a priestly community.

I am grateful to those who help us to exercise our communal priesthood by leading us in intercessions as specific as possible. Praying for "peace on earth" is a bit too abstract when, in fact, there is civil war in a specific country. Prayers for those who are grieving might better specifically name the community that has experienced terrible losses whether by storm or by a crazed killer. Praying for the sick in our own congregation is essential, just as it is to pray for the bereaved, since we are likely to know these people or to have exchanged the Peace with them, but when prayers are limited to praying for those who worship with us, it is easy to imagine that our caretaking need not extend beyond our own walls. Given that we are a people called to priestly service for "all the families of the earth," our praying needs to reach further. As our intercessions reach further, our awareness of the needs of others opens wider, and the broad extent of God's sympathies expands our own.

Saint John Chrysostom declared that prayers should be offered "for our neighbors, not only for the faithful, but for the unbelieving also."[10] Both Luther and Calvin were of the same mind. Calvin wrote, "Paul . . . tells the Ephesians to include all [people] in their prayers and not to restrict them to the body of the church . . . He not only bids us to pray for the salvation of unbelievers, but also to give thanks for their prosperity and well being."[11]

Not every evil that erupts in the world is traceable to some human cause, and its origins may be obscure. Sometimes the "cosmic powers of

---

10. McKee, "Calvin and Praying," 132.
11. Ibid., 133.

this present darkness," the "spiritual forces of evil" (Ephesians 6:12), weigh so heavily upon our neighbors that we have no effective defense to offer unless it be our prayers. In this way, as a priestly people, we both offer our solidarity with the distressed and summon our own hope in God as best we can for our neighbors' sake and for our own.

What Does Advocacy Look Like?

A priest is, at one and the same time, both intercessor and advocate. The church, as a corporate priesthood, not only prays for the poor, the vulnerable, the voiceless, and those likely to be mowed down by conflict, but also serves as an advocate on their behalf. Most are familiar, for example, with overtures enacted by governing bodies of various denominations speaking up for minorities of various sorts who find, not only social prejudice, but the law itself stacked against them. It is hard to know whether those denominational voices are ever heard or have any effect, but voices need to be raised nevertheless.

The Direct Action and Research Training Center (DART) is a network of congregation-based community organizations spread throughout twenty metropolitan areas in seven states. DART helps to gather local groups of congregations across the denominational spectrum to identify specific community issues that their representatives identify as priorities, and assists them in organizing to address those issues. Each local organization chooses an acronym to identify its mission. For example, in Lexington, Kentucky, the local organization is BUILD (Building a United Interfaith Lexington through Direct-Action), with a membership of twenty-two congregations: a diverse mix of persons of different races, economic classes, and religious traditions. They have worked on issues of affordable housing, health care for the uninsured, and drug treatment in jails, among others. Because they are a diverse body, and because they target specific, easily identifiable issues, they have frequently been successful.[12]

A similar organization in Richmond, Virginia, is called RISC (Richmonders Involved to Strengthen our Communities), representing twelve congregations of diverse backgrounds. RISC has had success working on issues related to the public schools. Partnering with public officials, RISC was successful in bringing down the truancy rate from 26 percent to 15 percent. RISC congregations also worked with the schools to guarantee that

---

12. See, for example, Direct Action & Research Training Center (DART). "BUILD."

students suspended multiple times receive an intervention with parents, teachers, and administrators.[13]

In Lexington, one issue for which there has not yet been a successful outcome is that of payday loans. Usually, a desperate borrower seeks such a loan to pay off other loans. If the borrower has a bank account, she has to grant the lender electronic access to it, or provide a postdated check that the company will cash on the client's next payday. Typically, these loans are intended to be short-term, to be repaid within two weeks. The finance charge on such loans is huge, accumulating to as much as 400 percent at an APR (annual percentage rate). Often a borrower is unable to repay a loan and so borrows again and then again, with interest accumulating at an unmanageable rate.

The Kentucky legislature, like many others, has permitted payday lenders to be exempted from usury laws, which used to cap short-term loans at 36 percent APR. The BUILD organization and its religious and secular allies in the Kentucky Coalition for Responsible Lending has so far been unsuccessful in persuading the legislature to limit the amount of interest on such loans, so the issue is ongoing, motivated by the understanding that the current laws do a disservice to desperate people who are often unaware of their options.

Some members of BUILD have drawn the attention of their denominational bodies to the issue of payday loans. One such body is the Kentucky-Indiana Synod of the ELCA, which has called upon its members to study the issue and make known to their legislators their opposition to abusive payday lending practices. Members of congregations in Indiana and Kentucky have even conducted protests in front of payday lending stores to draw public attention to the abuses of the payday lending industry. This sort of attentiveness to the poor is another example of the church finding ways to exercise its priestly role of intercessor and advocate.

Being Fed and Feeding Others

Of course, many congregations are involved either in ministries directly with the poor or in advocacy for vulnerable populations, all of which derive from the church's identity as a priestly people, whether or not the officers and members know that or think of it in those terms. Some congregations even link such ministries to the Eucharist, rediscovering that relationship

13. Direct Action & Research Training Center (DART), "RISC."

so embedded in early liturgical practice. Sara Miles, who, in her own words, "had led a thoroughly secular life, at best indifferent to religion, more often appalled by its fundamentalist crusades," walked into Saint Gregory of Nyssa Episcopal Church in San Francisco with unexpected results. "And so," she writes,

> I became a Christian, claiming a faith that many of my fellow believers want to exclude me from; following a God my unbelieving friends see as archaic superstition. At a time when Christianity in America is popularly represented by ecstatic teen crusaders in suburban megachurches, slick preachers proclaiming the 'gospel' of prosperity, and shrewd political organizers who rail against evolution, gay marriage, and stem-cell research, it's crucial to understand what faith actually means in the lives of people very different from one another.[14]

In time, Miles felt led to initiate a feeding ministry that begins at the very altar of her church, providing food for hundreds of people without their filling out any forms or the church's asking any questions.

Other congregations collect canned goods, or even loaves of bread, to be brought forward with the offering and deposited near the altar or table to be taken after the service to places where food is distributed or prepared and served to those who need it; still others commission members who will be taking their turn serving meals to or offering temporary shelter to homeless persons. The church's mission as a corporate priesthood and the duty to be attentive to the poor are profoundly linked, and lifting up these aspects of our ecclesial identity so that every member is aware of them and their relationship to each other must certainly help to identify who we are as disciples of Jesus Christ and what we are for—or better, *whom* we are for: the God who seeks a blessing for "all the families of the earth."

The Poor and the Protestant Ethic

Paying attention to the poor also requires defending the poor when they are wrongly blamed for their poverty. Blaming the poor for their poverty has always happened and frequently happens today. The irony is that some of those Americans who blame the poor for their situation do so under the banner of something that resembles the traditional Protestant ethic. Whether mainstream Protestants are praised or blamed for the Protestant

---

14. Miles, *Take This Bread*, xi and xiii.

ethic (now secularized as the *work* ethic), we need to reclaim it as our own, and not permit it to be distorted and used as a weapon against the poor.

The Protestant reformers were champions of an ethic rooted in the dignity of work. Work, however humble it might be, was understood to be a calling (a vocation), a service to God—and so it required personal discipline, honesty, and diligence. All of life involved living out one's vocation as a disciple of Jesus Christ, so it was important not only to work to support oneself and one's own family but also to plan ahead, save for the future, and to carry one's own weight. To live vocationally required learning the virtues of self-reliance, deferred gratification, and prudence. This so-called Protestant ethic, as rigorous as it sounds, was remarkably successful, and was honored, not only by Protestant Americans, but, in times past, became in effect the ethical default setting for the whole American culture, Protestant or not. Of course, it is an ethical system that can, in the hands of the unscrupulous, be used cynically for the purpose of exploiting those who have been schooled in it, and such exploitation is well documented in our history.

In the twenty-first century, those who oppose government safety nets for the poor have succumbed to the temptation to use their truncated version of the Protestant ethic to dignify their argument that the poor are likely to be at fault for their own poverty. In other words, if a person is poor, it is because she has not embraced the virtues required by the Protestant ethic, even though many of those who rely on public assistance are people who have jobs—often more than one. Even worse, the poor, including the working poor, have frequently been accused of deliberately gaming the system in order to get public support. A local television station or a national newspaper produces "undercover" stories to expose the "welfare queen," or people using food stamps to buy soft drinks that they can sell to get cash to buy drugs. No doubt there are such cheats, just as sometimes even lawyers or physicians commit much more lucrative white-collar crimes against public programs such as Medicare or Medicaid. The fact that cheating occurs among beneficiaries of very large public programs indicts the perpetrators, but has nothing to do with the much greater number, many of them children, whose need is beyond question.

The strengths of the Protestant ethic are strengths only when understood in their original context—a theological context that includes a sympathetic understanding of those whose life circumstances make it necessary to seek relief from the community, whether temporarily or permanently.

The Protestant ethic has not ignored the fact that there are circumstances that put people at a disadvantage, whether from birth or from the contingencies that present themselves in ordinary life, and they are not to be left alone in their distress.

Putting the Protestant Ethic in Theological Context

To blame the poor not only offers cover to those who want to cut government funding for those who are sick, out of work, or unable to compete in the job market, but it serves to bolster the illusion that it is possible, if one is virtuous enough, to escape from ever being thrust into a situation of dependency. Of course, there are some opponents of government programs for the poor who argue that taking care of the poor would be better done by charities, including through the benevolence of churches. Studies have shown that if every dime given to charity were to be given directly to the poor, the amount could not possibly fill the gap filled by SNAP (the Supplemental Nutritional Assistance Program—food stamps) alone. "No charity in the history of the planet could come up with the $80 billion for SNAP," said Ross Fraser, director of media relations for Feeding America . . . It doesn't make sense to talk about charity alone helping the hungry. It'd be like saying, why not let the military rely on charitable contributions."[15] Massive efforts by private charities during the Great Depression were insufficient to meet the need. "Agencies were struggling just to keep their doors open. In fact, between 1929 and 1932 about one-third of the nation's private agencies disappeared for lack of funds."[16] Yes, of course, churches and charities must be part of the answer, but they cannot serve as proxies to relieve the nation as a whole of its responsibility, either theoretically or practically; nor are they equipped to do so. The Protestant ethic is a worthy ethic when understood in a biblical and theological context but becomes cruel when that context is stripped away.

The theological context for what became known as the Protestant ethic is rooted in the Reformation, particularly in the influential work of both Luther and Calvin. These reformers believed that both the church and the state were obligated to take care of the poor and the vulnerable. Martin Luther praises Joseph for the creation of a national food assistance program in Egypt while he was in the service of Pharaoh.

15. Lubrano, "Charity," par. 17
16. Alliance for Children & Families, "Depression Era," par. 4.

As a counselor to Pharaoh, Joseph reminded him of the ruler's duty to insure that the necessities of life be made available to the people. 'It becomes the princes to provide for the poor,' Luther wrote, 'and especially those who are in their earliest years, lest they perish from hunger. Thus Joseph advised the king.'[17]

Luther also praised his own prince, Frederick of Saxony, who "'not only provided for public barns and granaries' and the preparation of field storage trenches but also ensured that grain and wine were stored in ample amount in the event of drought or pestilence."[18]

In a commentary on Psalm 82:3, John Calvin wrote, "a just and well-regulated government will be distinguished for maintaining the rights of the poor and afflicted . . . It is obvious why the cause of the poor and needy is here chiefly commended to rulers; for those who are exposed an easy prey to the cruelty and wrongs of the rich have no less need of the assistance and protection of magistrates than the sick have of the aid of the physician."[19]

In Luther's day, Leisnig, a Lutheran community southeast of Wittenberg, established a Community Chest for the poor. When donations were not sufficient, "the agreement mandated . . . an annual tax on every household in the town and parish, 'according to ability and means.'"[20] "Neither legitimate unemployment nor incapacity was to be stigmatized."[21] Calvin's city, Geneva, which gave shelter to thousands of religious refugees, set up a system of public works to provide a means of income for those in need. Christian concern for "the poor, the sick, the orphan, the widow, the refugee was institutionalized in the diaconate and legislated by law."[22] Geneva set up "a public *bourse* "to take care of the most striking examples of poverty, and the work of the public hospital was expanded to provide shelter, medical care, and work for the indigent and the refugee."[23]

Both Luther and Calvin permitted the charging of interest when a loan was made to provide the borrower with the use of venture capital rather than emergency support, but they believed that interest rates should be regulated so that the borrower would not be impoverished. Calvin certainly

---

17. Torvend, *Luther and the Hungry Poor*, 79.
18. Ibid., 87.
19. Calvin, *Opera*, 38, 769, 770, as cited in Graham, *Constructive Revolutiony*, 62.
20. Torvend, *Luther and the Hungry Poor*, 108.
21. Ibid., 111.
22. Graham, *Constructive Revolutiony*, 114.
23. Ibid., 65.

believed in commerce and in private poverty. He was no socialist. However, as Fred Graham puts it, "Calvin's thought helped produce a small welfare state in middle Europe in the sixteenth century."[24]

Losing the Theological Context

Marilynne Robinson, the novelist, has spent time reflecting on the sort of wisdom that is available in Calvin's work in particular. She sums up the catastrophe that results when the Protestant theology of work is torn out of its larger theological context. As she writes in *When I Was a Child*, "Jesus does *not* say, 'I was hungry and you fed me, though not in such a way as to interfere with free-market principles.'"[25]

When its theological context is lost, the Protestant ethic is reduced to a work ethic, as it has, of course, been renamed in our multicultural era. When the pious Lutheran or Calvinist loses his or her religious zeal, according to one observer, he or she quickly becomes "simply and unashamedly a rationalistic, remorseless pursuer of profit for its own sake."[26] One might add, such a person becomes ripe for conversion to an ideological sense of entitlement by the haves while conveniently recasting poverty of all sorts as indicative of moral fault and irresponsibility.

Protestants have no excuse for consenting to a politically popular ideology that demonizes the poor, while conveniently forgetting their own theological heritage, which points them in an entirely different direction. As a "priestly nation," the church of Jesus Christ needs to understand, honor, and cherish its role as intercessor and advocate for those from whom society would prefer to turn away. One part of advocacy is to follow the example of both Luther and Calvin in calling for "the prince"—i.e., those who govern—to take responsibility for providing an adequate safety net for those who, for whatever reason, face crises involving the lack of food, medical care, adequate shelter, and access to legal representation. Another part of it is to develop and support our own church-based ministries, some of direct service, others of advocacy, including the raising of a prophetic voice addressed to our own constituencies, the general community, and governing authorities. While most mainstream Protestant churches are already actively engaged in outreach projects and service to the community,

---

24. Ibid., 196.
25. Long, "Christian, Not Conservative."
26. Graham, *Constructive Revolutiony*, 192.

and often in lobbying government officials as well, it is important to be able to ground all these efforts theologically and liturgically rather than in a generic spirit of benevolence or civic responsibility alone.

When our worship provides for an offering for the poor every Lord's Day as the bridge between Word and Eucharist, joined to a broad range of intercessory prayer, the liturgy heightens consciousness of our identity as a priestly people. It is at this point that the biblical image of a communally shared churchly priesthood can help to bring into focus the identity of the baptized as a people whom God has chosen not for special privilege or favor but to be a "holy nation" whose purpose is to serve all of fragmented and contentious humankind. Such a theologically grounded image will, in many cases, call for an about-face—not so much calculating how well society or the ruling authorities are serving us, but rather turning toward both those persons and groups with whom we are in sympathy as well as those for whom sympathy comes hard, simply because this is our shared vocation in Christ, to whom we are apprenticed for life.

Epilogue

IS IT POSSIBLE FOR mainstream Protestantism to reposition itself in such a way as to escape being defined simplistically as the party shaped by indignant reaction to fundamentalism, on the one hand, or as those who have taken on the coloration of the dominant cultural skepticism on the other? Can it, without turning a deaf ear to contemporary culture—its questions and objections—set its own course on a trajectory guided by the inner logic and imperatives that flow from worship in Word and Sacrament, Scripture, the ecumenical creeds, and *episkopē*? Can it manage to reposition itself by rediscovering the affirmations at the heart of catholic and reforming Christianity, and thus avoid becoming co-opted by pervasive and often smothering cultural trends, or undermined by defensively clinging to paradigms that have become anachronistic? Can it recover an authoritative voice, claiming its identity as a mentoring community boldly affirming the triune God made known to us in Christ, a voice worthy of being taken seriously by thoughtful people? And can it reclaim its own biblical and theological heritage when some have recast its ethic to use as a cudgel with which to attack the poor and vulnerable?

The church has met awesome challenges before as it has encountered new cultures and changes in old ones. The challenge in our time is, of course, unique to us. I believe it is a challenge that can strengthen and encourage the church. It begins, I think, with a conversation—one that includes, as best we can, the saints with whom the conversation began, along with those who are living and whose voices should be expected to weigh in. It is a conversation that calls for a measure of trust, if we can manage such a thing—trust in the greater church: ecumenical, catholic, reforming—but most of all, trust in the providence of the holy God who speaks with an authority the church can only partially and feebly represent, a God who, however fragile our own testimony, will certainly have the last word.

A Sermon Preached at First Presbyterian Church, Lexington, Kentucky, on the Fourth Sunday after Pentecost, Year A of the Revised Common Lectionary

July 6, 2014: Matthew 11:16–19, 25–30

JULY 4 REMINDS US that Americans are, by and large, a people who have a hard time with authority. Any kind of authority—you name it. The authority of kings and parliaments. The authority of presidents and legislatures and Supreme Courts. The authority of dad or mom or your math teacher. The authority of those with enough spare cash to buy the political outcome that serves their interests. The authority of bishops and elders and ministers and General Assemblies. We've learned at our mother's knees, though sometimes unintentionally, to be both skeptical and suspicious. We do not easily grant authority to anyone. Some of you may remember those bumper stickers from the '60s and '70s: "Question Authority."

It's not a bad idea to be careful deciding whom to trust. But, on the other hand, it can't be healthy not to trust anybody ever. Once you give yourself over to a thoroughly skeptical frame of mind, you can build a case against anyone.

John the Baptist attracted huge crowds. He caught people's attention and some of them took him seriously. But his words were sharp, and he offended the kind of people who can be dangerous when offended. Naturally, his detractors found ways to discredit him. Look at John, after all: he didn't dress like anybody you ever knew—you'd be embarrassed if your friends saw you hanging out with him. Didn't eat like everybody else. Wouldn't recognize a quarter pounder if he saw one. He was too ascetic, too abstemious, nobody you'd want to have lunch with.

If it was easy for detractors to build a case against John, it was just as easy to build a case against Jesus—but you had to turn the complaint all the way around, inside out, and upside down. If John lived like a hermit, Jesus could be blamed for being just the opposite. Jesus's detractors discredited him because he was happy to sit down at anyone's table for a meal. "For John came neither eating nor drinking, and they say, 'He has a demon'; the Son of Man came eating and drinking, and they say, 'Look, a glutton and a drunkard, a friend of tax collectors and sinners!'" In other words, you're damned if you do, and damned if you don't.

We are a people suspicious of authority, and maybe especially suspicious of religious authority. In our time, a lot of people identify themselves as "spiritual, but not religious." "Spiritual," I suppose, because hardly anybody wants to believe that we human beings are nothing but walking computers made out of meat. "Not religious," I guess, because we worry that being "religious" means apprenticing ourselves to some authority.

In the church, the authority we have to deal with is the authority of Jesus Christ, a Galilean Jew around whom God has gathered a people, the church. A mixed bag of folk, for better or worse. Confucius and Buddha and Mohammed may or may not interest us, but in the church we have to deal with this particular Jew, this Jesus. Because for the church his voice is not just one voice among many voices. For the church, his voice is the decisive voice, the critically urgent voice, a voice that calls us to pay specific and careful attention. It's a hard thing to pay attention to his voice, his particular voice, when there are so many loud voices already in our ears; a hard thing to spare him a hearing when our skepticism is working overtime. A hard thing to do when we're constantly on guard against the fraud, the scam artist, the snake oil salesman.

We are "spiritual, not religious," and we're trying to work something out all by ourselves, maybe by borrowing a little feng shui here, a little Dr. Phil there. How's that working out for you? Would we recognize an authoritative voice if we heard one? If there should actually be some voice addressing us, some voice from the very center of the universe, would we give it a moment's attention?

In today's reading, Matthew reports Jesus to be saying that God has reached out to us, revealing mysteries as important as your life is important. And he says there are some people who "get it," and others who don't "get it." No explanation as to why this should be so. Except for a non-explanatory explanation. As Jesus puts it, God has "hidden these things from the wise and the intelligent and . . . revealed them to infants." I suspect that when he refers to the "wise and intelligent" who don't "get it," he's speaking tongue in cheek. What he really means by "the wise and intelligent" are those who define themselves in those terms. They are self-assessed as "wise and intelligent." They are the ones who imagine that they're smarter, shrewder, more likely to be in-the-know than anybody else. On the other hand, those who really do "get it"—the so-called infants—are those who are less likely to think they already know it all.

And what is this mystery that's been revealed? Is it a body of information, a collection of facts, some inside secrets that explain everything? I don't think so. What's been revealed to those with the simplicity to recognize it is not how to get the universe under your control, or how to invest wisely and come out on top, nor is it seven secrets to success in love or business. The mystery God has revealed is a person: Jesus himself. "No one knows the Father except the Son and anyone to whom the Son chooses to reveal him." In other words, Jesus comes from the very heart of God, and in him the very heart of God has been opened to us.

The question remains: since we're inclined to be "spiritual, but not religious" . . . since we're inclined to be suspicious of any voice of authority . . . how can we trust the voice of Jesus just because our Sunday school teacher told us to?

Jesus recognizes the conundrum. If it's possible to be skeptical of the voice of one who lives a stripped-down life in the desert, on the one hand; and, on the other hand, equally possible to be skeptical of the voice of one who sits down for a meal anytime, anywhere, even with outcasts: if skepticism is the default setting, no matter what, how do we trust anyone? Here's what Jesus said, as Matthew recalls it: "Wisdom is vindicated by her deeds." I know, that's clear as mud. But I think it really isn't all that hard. It means, more or less, that when it comes to authority, you know it when you see it.

And here's what I see and hear when I lift my eyes from that tiny screen it's so hard to take my eyes off of and take a long look at Jesus: I see one who says, "Come to me, all you that are weary and are carrying heavy burdens, and I will give you rest. Take my yoke upon you, and learn from me, for I am gentle and humble in heart, and you will find rest for your souls." He says that, and he demonstrates what gentleness and humility look like when he heals the sick, feeds the hungry, rebukes those who oppress the poor and vulnerable, and speaks up for those who don't even dare to raise their own voices.

And contrast that invitation with the one you don't hear. You don't hear him saying, "I want you to join such-and-such a church, and help them meet their goal of 250 new members by Christmas." He doesn't say, "Give me your money and I'll make sure you can afford to buy a Lamborghini." He doesn't say, "Let's all get together and figure out who to hate." He's not saying, "Everybody's going to hell but you."

Some folks get it. And I don't know any way to speculate about who's going to get it and who isn't going to get it. But I'm pretty sure that those who think gentleness and humility are a joke will not get it. And such folk are not rare these days, or any days. Rodney Stark says that pagan philosophy "regarded mercy and pity as pathological emotions—defects of character to be avoided by all rational [people] . . . a defect of character unworthy of *the wise*."[1] Once upon a time, Americans gave at least lip service to honoring gentleness and humility. We still admire it in tributes you hear at funerals. But for most practical purposes, gentleness and humility are off the table. With or without our participation, society is teaching our children to be tough, competing ruthlessly for tangible rewards—the kind you can count and add up. If the bottom line says you have to fire a thousand people and send their jobs to China to increase the price of your stock by a nickel, you do it. If you have to betray a friend to secure a place on the team or become valedictorian, the savvy advice says, "Go for it."

So, if Jesus represents another way of life than "winner take all," he's already lost a lot of friends and is bound to lose more. But he won't lose *all* his friends, because even those who think gentleness and humility is a joke, a sickness, a loser's game, may be moved by it when they see it. Or moved by it when they desperately need at least a teaspoon of gentleness and humility just to pick them up off the floor.

Some of you are carrying heavy burdens—burdens you'd rather the rest of us not know about. Some of you are tired with a kind of tiredness that won't be fixed by getting a good night's sleep or even taking a month off. To you, and to anyone who's in a position to hear his voice, Jesus says, "Come to me, all you that are weary and are carrying heavy burdens, and I will give you rest." Come on, you folks who are cobbling together some kind of spirituality, all on your own, and not getting very far with it. Come, apprentice yourself to me. I know you better than you know yourself. "Take

---

1. Stark, *Rise of Christianity*, 212, quoted in Torvend, *Luther and the Hungry Poor*, 37 (my italics).

my yoke upon you and learn from me . . ." Learn what? Learn gentleness; learn humility. And, "you will find rest for your souls."

Is that easy work, do you think? Being apprenticed to this guy, who asks us to turn our faces toward the ignored, the left out, and the sick at heart? Toward the kinds of people Ayn Rand despises? Not easy work. Not easy, but then, easy: "My yoke is easy, and my burden is light." Because doing whatever you have to do turns out not to be just a burden when there's love mixed into it. Sitting up with a sick child. Hard. Hard . . . But easy. Standing up for a friend in trouble. Hard . . . But easy. Factoring in people and their spouses and kids when you're calculating the bottom line. A hard thing to do . . . But hard things can feel easy when this One has your back. "Come . . . Take my yoke upon you, and learn from me . . . For my yoke is easy, and my burden is light."

> Now to the One who by the power at work within us
> is able to do far more abundantly than all we can ask or imagine,
> to God be glory in the church and in Christ Jesus
> to all generations, forever and ever.

Bibliography

Alliance for Children & Families. "Depression Era Further Defines Movement." In *A Century of Service*. Online: http://alliance1.org/centennial/book/depression-era-further-defines-movement-1930s/.
Bendroth, Margaret. *The Spiritual Practice of Remembering*. Grand Rapids: Eerdmans, 2013.
Brooks, David. "The Mental Virtues." *New York Times*, August 29, 2014. Online: http://www.nytimes.com/2014/08/29/opinion/david-brooks-the-mental-virtues.html?_r=0
Byars, Ronald P. *The Sacraments in Biblical Perspective*. Interpretation: Resources for the Use of Scripture in the Church. Louisville: Westminster John Knox, 2011.
———. *What Language Shall I Borrow? The Bible and Christian Worship*. Calvin Institute of Christian Worship Liturgical Studies Series. Grand Rapids: Eerdmans, 2008.
Calvin, John. *Institutes of the Christian Religion*. Edited by John T. McNeill. 2 vols. Library of Christian Classics 20–21. Philadelphia: Westminster, 1960.
———. *Opera quae supersunt omnia*. Vol. 38. Edited by Guillaume Baum et al. Corpus Reformatorum. Brunswick: n.p., 1863–1900.
Campbell, Ted A. "Glory Days? The Myth of the Mainline." *Christian Century*, July 9 (2014) 11–13. Online: http://www.christiancentury.org/article/2014-06/glory-days/.
Craddock, Fred B. *Luke*. Interpretation: A Bible Commentary for Teaching and Preaching. Louisville: John Knox, 1990.
Direct Action & Research Training Center (DART). "BUILD." Online: http://www.thedartcenter.org/location/build/.
———. "RISC." Online: http://www.thedartcenter.org/location/risc/.
Driel, Edwin Chr. van. "The World Is about to Turn: Retelling the Story of Jesus Eschatologically." *Call to Worship: Liturgy, Music, Preaching, and the Arts* 46/4 (2013) 23–27.
Ellul, Jacques. *The False Presence of the Kingdom*. Translated by C. Edward Hopkin. New York: Seabury, 1972.
Episcopal Church. *The Book of Common Prayer and Administration of the Sacraments and Other Rites and Ceremonies of the Church according to the Use of the Episcopal Church*. New York: The Church Hymnal Corporation, 1979.
Evangelical Lutheran Church in America. *Evangelical Lutheran Worship*. Minneapolis: Augsburg Fortress, 2006.
Gopnik, Adam. "Bigger Than Phil." *New Yorker*, February 17 & 24, 2014, 107–12. Online: http://www.newyorker.com/magazine/2014/02/17/bigger-phil/.

Graham, W. Fred. *The Constructive Revolutionary: John Calvin & His Socio-Economic Impact*. Richmond, VA: John Knox, 1971.

Johnson, Maxwell E. *Praying and Believing in Early Christianity: The Interplay between Christian Worship and Doctrine*. Collegeville, MN: Liturgical, 2013.

Jungmann, Josef. *The Mass of the Roman Rite: Its Origins and Development*. Translated by Francis A. Brunner. Revised by Charles K. Riepe. New revised and abridged ed. New York: Benziger, 1959.

Lathrop, Gordon W. *The Four Gospels on Sunday: The New Testament and the Reform of Christian Worship*. Minneapolis: Fortress, 2012.

———. *Holy Things: A Liturgical Theology*. Minneapolis: Fortress, 1993.

Leith, John H., ed. *Creeds of the Churches: A Reader in Christian Doctrine from the Bible to the Present*. 3rd ed. Atlanta: John Knox, 1982.

Long, Robert. "Christian, Not Conservative." October 15, 2013. Online: http://www.theamerican-conservative.com/articles/christian-not-conservative/.

Lubrano, Alfred. "Charity Can't Fill Holes in Aid to Poor." May 2, 2013. Online: http://articles.philly.com/2013-05-02/news/38960249_1_charity-hunger-special-supplemental-nutrition-program/.

McDonald, Lee Martin. *Formation of the Bible: The Story of the Church's Canon*. Peabody, MA: Hendrickson, 2012.

McKee, Elsie. "Calvin and Praying for 'All People Who Dwell on Earth.'" *Interpretation* 63 (2009) 130–40.

Miles, Sara. *Take This Bread: A Radical Conversion*. New York: Ballantine, 2007.

Mitchell, Nathan. "The Amen Corner: Being Good and Being Beautiful." *Worship* 74 (2000) 550–58.

Pitts, Leonard, Jr. "Taking Selfies in the Wrong Places." *Miami Herald*, July 26, 2014. Online: http://www.miamiherald.com/2014/07/26/4255141/leonard-pitts-jr-taking-selfies.html/.

Presbyterian Church (U.S.A). *Book of Common Worship*. Louisville: Westminster/John Knox, 1993.

Presbyterian Church (U.S.A.). *Glory to God: The Presbyterian Hymnal*. Louisville: Westminster John Knox, 2013.

Ross, Michael S. "Young Minds in Critical Condition." *New York Times*, The Opinion Pages. May 11, 2014. Online: http://opinionator.blogs.nytimes.com/2014/05/10/young-minds-in-critical-condition/.

Rutledge, Fleming. *And God Spoke to Abraham: Preaching from the Old Testament*. Grand Rapids: Eerdmans, 2011.

Smith, James K. A. *Imagining the Kingdom: How Worship Works*. Cultural Liturgies. Grand Rapids: Baker Academic, 2013.

Soulen, R. Kendall. *The Divine Name(s) and the Holy Trinity*. Vol. 1, *Distinguishing the Voices*. Louisville: Westminster John Knox, 2011.

Stark, Rodney. *The Rise of Christianity: How the Obscure, Marginal Jesus Movement Became the Dominant Religious Force in the Western World in a Few Centuries*. San Francisco: HarperSanFrancisco, 1997.

Thompson, Bard. *Liturgies of the Western Church*. Philadelphia: Fortress, 1961.

Torvend, Samuel. *Luther and the Hungry Poor: Gathered Fragments*. Minneapolis: Fortress. 2008.

United Methodist Church (U.S.A.). *The United Methodist Book of Worship*. Nashville: United Methodist Publishing House, 1992.

Wiman, Christian. *My Bright Abyss: Meditation of a Modern Believer*. New York: Farrar, Straus and Giroux, 2013.

www.ingramcontent.com/pod-product-compliance
Lightning Source LLC
Chambersburg PA
CBHW020855160426
43192CB00007B/937